Beard on Pasta

Beard on Pasta

a James Beard Cookbook

Drawings by Karl W. Stuecklen

WINGS BOOKS

New York • Avenel, New Jersey

Some of these recipes originally appeared in *Woman's Day*.

This 1994 edition is published by Wings Books,
distributed by Random House Value Publishing, Inc.,
40 Engelhard Avenue, Avenel, New Jersey 07001,
by arrangement with Alfred A. Knopf, Inc.

Random House
New York • Toronto • London • Sydney • Auckland

Printed and bound in the United States of America

Library of Congress Cataloging-in-Publication Data
Beard, James, 1903–
Beard on pasta/by James Beard; drawings by Karl W. Stuecklen.
p. cm.
Originally published: New York : Knopf : distributed by Random House, 1983
Includes index.
ISBN 0-517-11927-7
1. Cookery (Pasta) I. Title
TX809.M17B4 1994
641.8'22—dc20   94-21596
                                                      CIP

8 7 6 5 4 3 2

TO BEATRICE PETERSON
a great teacher and good friend

Contents

Introduction

This is a book of good times to have with pasta.

I never get tired of pasta, any more than I get tired of bread. I eat it when I'm exhausted and want a quick meal that will give me a lift. I eat it when I'm in an ambitious mood, looking for something pleasant and different to compliment a guest.

When I want something spicy, I toss spaghetti with warm olive oil, garlic, and anchovies. When I want something voluptuous, I bake elbow macaroni in a cheese-rich béchamel sauce. And, when I'm fed up with complicated foods, I fill a bowl with piping-hot green noodles and cover them with icy tomatoes and scallions in a sharp vinaigrette.

Pasta is always the same, yet always different. It has a comforting familiarity, with its pale golden color and chewy, wheaten taste. And then there are all those amusing shapes, and the thousands of ways to sauce them: from avocado to zucchini, or from plain butter and cheese to purée of frogs' legs.

It's always different because we find pasta recipes in nearly every country in the world. I should say right at the start that this isn't an Italian cookbook. It's a collection of worldwide noodle dishes that I like and like to make. There are Italian recipes in it. But there are also dishes from Germany, France, China, and Greece. There are a kosher-style noodle pudding and an English macaroni dessert.

In my own life, pasta didn't begin as an Italian food at all. I must have been six or seven before I ever ate spaghetti, but I was eating Chinese noodles long before that.

They were given to me by Let, the Chinese chef who worked for my mother. He used to make a soup that was a rather weak chicken stock absolutely full of noodles, ham, scallions, and thin strips of egg that he had beaten up, cooked in a thin pancake, and then sliced into strips.

We went fairly often to Chinese restaurants in Portland, and I loved the chow mein and fried noodles. It was nothing like the chow mein on beds of crisp little twigs that you get now. It was more like lo mein. The noodles were boiled and then quickly fried so that they were brown and crispy on the bottom, and they would be covered with shredded vegetables and cubes of tofu.

I didn't have Italian noodles until I was in school, when we started going to a pretty good Italian restaurant that served "family-style" meals at great long tables. They'd bring you a little antipasto and then a dish of pasta. The menu never varied, and it was always fifty cents. They made a good tomato sauce, and one with butter and fresh herbs, and a version of carbonara. The sauces were nothing complicated, but it was great fun, and I just loved it; and, after all, what can you do for fifty cents?

Oddly enough, when I began to cook pasta myself, it was in the German style. That was because my mother had close friends who were from a German family, and they used noodles a lot in soups and with stews. They had one wonderful dish for which they took all the lesser parts of the pig—the backbone and the tail and such—braised them, and served them with sauerkraut and noodles. That was fun.

The point of all these reminiscences is to show how, even in a small American city at the beginning of this century, there were several quite distinct traditions of cooking with pasta.

I don't know where the historians will eventually tell us pasta started. I'm sure, however, that the old romantic notion that Marco Polo came back to Venice from China toting the secret of spaghetti has been pretty much debunked.

My guess is that we will never find a starting place for pasta, because it will turn out to have popped up in several different places, all quite independent of one another, and then to have been carried along the trade routes by camel, ship, and peddler's pack.

You just have to look at rice noodles and mung-bean noodles to see that the Oriental tradition is quite separate from ours. Or to consider the very early Bulgarian pasta—lumps of dried dough that horsemen carried in their saddlebags and grated into pots of boiling milk at the end of the day's ride.

We do know that there is a long history around the Eastern Mediterranean of making simple wheat doughs for boiling. We know that noodles were being sold in Greece as early as the fifth century. Pasta in Italy probably started in the south, as part of that whole Mediterranean culture. We know that the Romans grew wheat in Sicily; and what better way is there to preserve wheat flour than to make it into a paste and dry it?

Yet the first Italian references to pasta are terribly offhanded. A legal document mentions that someone has inherited a basket of macaroni or a sieve for draining noodles. Or a saint's legend tells how the devil was foiled in his scheme to fill a virtuous man's pasta with dirt. It seems that the saint was present at that meal. When he said the blessing over the food, the dirt was transformed into sweet ricotta, and everyone enjoyed a good dinner. What a wonderfully Italian miracle that one was!

It's just because pasta is part of the cooking of so many different cultures that we don't have to feel bound by the rules of any one country when we cook it. That's why I've made no attempt in this book to be particularly classical or traditional. My aim here, as in all my books and teaching, is to encourage pleasure and individual taste in the way we eat.

Of course there are well-established rules in Italy about the right way to serve and eat pasta. These are customs that have grown out of centuries of experience, and they have the authority of a lot of good eating behind them.

In the question of matching pasta to sauce, for example, the Italians can be very specific. Marcella Hazan says to use thin spaghetti for seafood sauces, regular spaghetti for cream sauces. Giuliano Bugialli says you should try always to serve pesto sauce on trenette, a flat, narrow noodle.

But we're Americans, with a whole melting pot of cultures behind us, and we don't have to do things the classic Italian way. We can do as we please.

When we pick a pasta to go with a sauce, we feel free to experiment and discover what appeals to us. Once we've chosen our sauce, we try to imagine how it will taste. What pasta would go well with it? Will it take a chewy ziti, delicate angel hair, or ricelike orzo?

We may find, eventually, that certain pastas seem right with certain sauces. That tubular shapes, like penne, and envelope shapes, like seashells, seem right when a sauce has tiny bits of meat or fish to be caught in the spaces. That fine, slender noodles seem proper with thin tomato sauces. That we want a good chewy twist to stand up to a cold pasta salad full of cheese and broccoli.

But you shouldn't take this on anyone's authority, least of all mine.

Instead, consult your own taste and style, and feel free to experiment. Take chances. We Americans have been intimidated for far too long by other people's opinions on what we should eat.

We've been even more intimidated, I think, in the area of table manners and propriety. Pasta is not a mannerly food to eat. And I remember when hostesses in this country were so insecure and etiquette-conscious that they would break up noodles into inch-long pieces before they cooked them, and would choose elbow macaroni over spaghetti so that their guests wouldn't risk the crime of slurping at the table.

I think we've gotten over that kind of tearoom niceness, but now there is another worry people have about eating pasta, which is of not doing things in the proper Italian way. They worry about whether the Italians use bowls or plates, and whether it's proper to serve a soupspoon along

with the fork as a help in picking up the strands, and how to avoid slurping up the last inches of long noodles.

To which I say that it's time to stop worrying and start enjoying.

Shallow bowls are nice to have, and they make it easier to pick up the pasta. But, if you don't have them, then plates are fine. Remember that the Chinese hold a small bowl under their chins and shovel the noodles into their mouths with their chopsticks.

Do you serve a spoon alongside your spaghetti? Italians say that only children, the infirm, and the ill-mannered use soupspoons as props for their forks when picking up pasta. I think spoons serve a more important function, that of getting up the sauce left at the bottom of the bowl. I've often wiped up the last flavorful puddle of oil and garlic with a crust of bread, which was a good, if starchy, solution. But if you have a soupspoon, you can capture the last cream-covered peas and prosciutto, the last basil-flavored tomato sauce or capers in olive oil from the bottom of the bowl.

As for picking up the pasta, use the spoon if it helps. The Italians have perfected a technique for picking up long noodles on a fork. They stick the fork into the mass of pasta and twirl it around one or two times until they have a neat amount of pasta wrapped around the tines. One warning: experienced eaters are careful to start with just a few strands of noodles on their forks, or else they wind up with a package that is larger than their mouths can accommodate.

How do you deal with the short strands that are left hanging from your mouth? Without embarrassment, certainly. It's bound to happen when spaghetti is cooked just right, because only overcooked pasta is soft and pliable enough to form a tidy package around the fork. A few luscious strands are bound to hang loose, and must be taken into the mouth as skillfully as possible. If you slurp them, so be it. Because the truly best way, the only classical and true way, to eat pasta is with gusto.

OBSERVATIONS

Commercial Dried Pastas
(Italian and domestic · egg noodles
Chinese dried noodles · specialty noodles)
Store-Bought Fresh Pasta
Flour for Homemade Pasta
Equipment for Making and Saucing Pasta
(mixing · rolling · shaping
extrusion machines)
Cooking Pasta
Portions
Important Ingredients
(tomatoes · olive oil · cheese)
What to Drink with Pasta

Commercial Dried Pastas

ITALIAN AND DOMESTIC

I'm a great fan of good commercial pasta made with durum wheat. It has a mellow flavor and strong texture that are standards for what good pasta should be.

The clue is in the words "durum wheat" or, on the Italian package, "pura semolina." You have to read the ingredients on the package, and buy only pasta that is made with durum-wheat flour. I recently had both American and Italian dried shells, and I could find no difference between the two.

Most, although by no means all, of the Italian commercial brands are pretty good. De Cecco maintains a tremendously high quality and produces hundreds of different shapes. But I've also had Italian dried pasta that was no good at all.

Among American dried pastas, I've always found that Buitoni makes a damned good product. It's not fair, however, to name one brand, because there are so many small pasta manufacturers all over the country, wherever there is an Italian population. Every so often I am invited to the Macaroni Luncheon in New York City (and I go with pleasure, because you get a first-rate meal there). All the small local factory owners are introduced and asked to say a few words, and I can tell you that these introductions last throughout the whole meal. With American dried pastas, as with the Italian, you just have to become ingredient conscious, and choose only brands made with durum flour.

Just now, we are in the midst of a kind of snobbery: people think that any fresh pasta is better than any dried pasta. That just isn't so. There is nothing wrong with good commercial pasta; in many cases it is better than the fresh pasta you can buy.

EGG NOODLES

Your supermarket probably has several brands of home-style egg noodles in boxes and cellophane bags, many of them with German or Pennsylvania Dutch names. Some of them are pretty good, as long as you use them for the dishes they were designed for. Use them for noodle pudding, for Pork with Sauerkraut Noodles, or for Alsatian chicken and noodles. You'll be disappointed if you try to use them in an Italian dish.

CHINESE AND JAPANESE DRIED NOODLES

In recent years, New York has become studded with hundreds of tiny produce stores run by Korean immigrants. In addition to selling broccoli and oranges, most of them stock a few Oriental specialties, such as udon, buckwheat, rice, and mung-bean noodles. I've found all the brands to be quite reliable, although perhaps I don't bring to them the educated palate that I do to Western pastas. Just be sure to use them properly.

Rice noodles, made from ground rice, are more fragile than wheat noodles. They need a brief soaking before you cook them. Mung-bean noodles are made from powdered mung beans. They too have to be soaked, after which they are gelatinous and springy. They don't actually need any cooking at all after their soaking, but can be briefly stir-fried, the way you do bean sprouts. Udon and buckwheat noodles act like American wheat noodles.

SPECIALTY NOODLES

I buy dried whole-wheat pasta in health-food stores, and I just love it. It's not only the color but the special nearly meaty chewiness that I find appealing. And for many years I have enjoyed De Boles artichoke pasta, which is not made, as you might suspect, from globe artichokes, but from Jerusalem artichokes. It's quite delicious, and it's good for people who can't eat wheat for one reason or another. De Boles also makes a corn pasta that is delicious, but both are very hard to come by.

Store-Bought Fresh Pasta

The best fresh commercial noodles I've ever had are the ones I buy in New York's Chinatown. They are made with flour and water, and come in just a few shapes. You buy them soft, packed in plastic bags, and should store them in the refrigerator. They are well worth going out of your way for.

In certain cities one can now find several grades of fresh pasta. In New York for several years we have had a standard, a wonderful pasta from a maker called Raffetto. Now Marcella Hazan is overseeing the production of some topnotch pasta that is sold fresh at Bloomingdale's. She is very particular about using only durum wheat and fresh eggs, and her pasta couldn't be better.

But just because pasta is fresh doesn't guarantee that it's going to be good. There is now so-called fresh pasta that is sold in cardboard trays in supermarkets far inferior to good dried pasta. This is one occasion when freshness does not ensure quality. I believe it's far better to use a first-rate dried pasta made of durum-wheat flour than a trendy, mushy brand that dissolves in the water like a dumpling.

Flour for Homemade Pasta

All the recipes in this book were tested with all-purpose flour, because that's the kind you can buy in your supermarket. But it isn't the best flour for making pasta by any means. The best you can get is hard-wheat flour, sometimes called *durum flour, pasta flour,* or, in England, *strong wheat flour.*

All wheat flour contains a protein called gluten. It's the gluten in the wheat that gives tension and elasticity to dough. Durum-wheat flour has more gluten than ordinary flour, and it makes not only the best pasta, but also the best bread. A dough made with durum flour will be noticeably easier to knead and to roll out than one made with all-purpose flour.

It's not easy to find hard-wheat flour, although we're beginning to see it sold in large cities. You may find it in health-food stores or order it from mail-order houses. It's worth looking out for, because there is really no comparison between pasta that is made with supermarket all-purpose flour and the firm, flavorful high-quality pasta made with hard-wheat flour.

(Semolina in the United States is coarsely ground hard wheat, less fine and more granular in texture than hard-wheat flour. One doesn't usually find semolina here except in Italian markets, usually in bags imported from Italy. I use it mostly for dishes such as gnocchi and spätzle and sometimes to make bread. I have made pasta with it, but don't try using it in an extrusion machine—it will clog up the works.)

But don't worry if you can't get durum flour, because the recipes in the book were designed to work with ordinary all-purpose flour, which is actually a blend of soft and hard wheats. Just remember that you can't count on flour having a standard quality. For a while, General Mills was selling an all-purpose flour that was supposed to be the same all over the country. Even so, it varied with age and with the temperature in the market and in home kitchens. That's why you may sometimes have to add a little extra oil or a tablespoonful or two of flour to get your dough to the proper consistency.

Equipment for Making and Saucing Pasta

MIXING

You can get a good dough every time using either an *electric mixer* or the *food processor*. But it isn't difficult to mix by hand: it's the kneading that takes all the work. For hand mixing, you just need a *work space* and a *fork*.

Dough scrapers are useful for cleaning off the board after you've combined the flour and eggs to make the dough.

ROLLING

If there is one piece of pasta-making equipment I wouldn't want to be without, it is my Bialetti *pasta-rolling machine*. It works on the principle of the wringer, squeezing the dough between two cylindrical plastic rollers until it is paper thin. I have the motor-driven machine, which makes an infernal racket but produces good noodles, and I just love it. I know people who own the hand-cranked rolling machine and like the sense of control they get with it. The hand machine is a lot cheaper and infinitely quieter than the motor-driven machine, and as far as I can tell, one is as good as the other when it comes to rolling and cutting the dough. If you're going to spend any money on this business of making pasta, this is where you will want to do it.

If you're rolling by hand, you should know about the special long *rolling pin* made for pasta. It's about three feet long, and is the same width all the way down. (My guess is that it was modeled after the broomsticks

that people have used for years to roll pasta.) According to Marcella Hazan, this pin should be hung vertically for storage so that it doesn't warp. I brought one home from Italy years ago. It's thinner than the classic wooden pin—about 1½ to 2 inches in diameter—and I have trouble using it because my hands are too big.

When you roll the dough by hand, you'll need a good *work space*. Marble is perfect for it, but of course wood works very well, and is the traditional surface in Italy. Many people like to use a *pastry cloth* as a kind of security blanket against sticky dough, but I've never felt the need of one.

When you're rolling the pasta, you might want to have a big soft *brush* on hand for dusting it with flour, just as you would when you make puff pastry.

And, while we're talking of rolling by hand, let me say that good, strong stomach muscles are a help, so that you can lean your tummy against one end of the sheet of pasta while you're rolling and stretching the other end. And arm muscles, too, are helpful for dealing with a properly stiff dough!

SHAPING

You can cut out the noodles with your small *rolling machine*, simply by changing from the smooth rollers to the cutting rollers. Or you can fold up the sheets of dough and then cut them with a sharp *knife*. But it's helpful to have a *rolling blade*, straight-edged or wavy, of the sort that is used to cut out ravioli, pastry strips, and pizza slices.

EXTRUSION MACHINES

It was inevitable that the manufacturers would copy the pasta industry and produce small extrusion machines for the home kitchen. By extrusion, we mean machines that push the dough through a die so that it comes out with a shape.

There are two kinds. With the first, you still mix your dough in the traditional manner, either in the electric mixer or the food processor. Then you put it into a container, from which it is pushed through shaping dies. This is the method used in the Kitchen Aid, Cuisinart, and Robot-Coupe extrusion machines.

In the other machines, such as the Simac, Bialetti, and Osrow (and there may be more on the market by the time this is printed), you simply put flour and eggs in the opening at the top of the machine and, after a suitable amount of time has passed for kneading and processing, the pasta comes out the other end.

The one thing these machines give you that few people have ever had before is absolutely fresh round and tubular pasta. That's because, even in Italy, pasta that is formed by extrusion is always made in factories and sold dried.

I suppose that we have to take it for granted that these machines are going to be part of our lives, and to hope that they will at least introduce

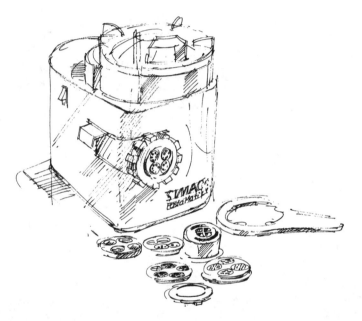

homemade pasta to people who would never dare to make it in any other way. They turn out a reliable product, and they do their job in less than five minutes.

I have a few reservations about them, nonetheless. I'm not sure that they produce as flavorful a pasta, or pasta with as good a texture as we can get by traditional methods, owing to the fact that the manufacturers recommend that you use soft-wheat or cake flour. While the product looks and acts the same, you just aren't going to get the flavor from cake flour that you will get from good hard-wheat flour. But hard-wheat flour tends to clog the dies of the machines.

And, although the machines are time-savers in one sense, they eat up time later on. If you use a small die, it takes a great deal of time to get it spotlessly clean. You have to poke out every crumb of dried dough from the die, or it won't work properly the next time you use it. When I tried one of the machines, it took me nearly an hour to worry out all the caked-up dough left in the dies. The manufacturer had even provided a little double-edged toothpick for the job!

As I write this, we're just in the beginning of the development of the new machines. Who knows how they will be improved once thousands of pasta makers get to working with them? But at the moment my opinion is that you can't do better than to mix the dough in the mixer or food processor and then put it through a small rolling machine. You'll have a beautiful pasta with superior texture and taste.

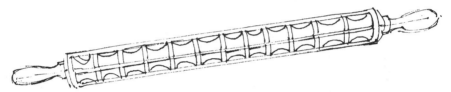

For making ravioli, I have a *marked rolling pin*. You roll it over a sheet of dough and it marks squares on the sheet. You put dabs of filling in the squares on half the dough, fold the other marked half over it, and then cut along the lines with a knife or rolling blade.

I've also used *ravioli trays*, metal trays with shallow indentations in them. You lay the dough over the tray, and drop bits of filling into the hollows. Cover them with a second sheet of dough, and run a rolling pin over it all.

You can buy round or square *tortellini stamps* that work like cookie cutters. As a matter of fact, if you have a round cookie cutter, use that instead.

I own two *spätzle-making machines.* Both work by passing a blade over large holes in the bottom of a round or rectangular container. You put the dough into the container, and it is cut off by the blade at regular intervals and falls into boiling water.

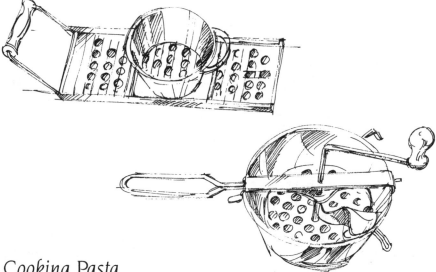

Cooking Pasta

Although I've been cooking pasta nearly all my life, the one thing I can't begin to tell you is how long it is going to take. The time varies too much, depending on the heat of the day, the amount of water in the pot, the kind of flour used, the proportion of flour to liquid in the dough, the shape of the noodles, and how long the pasta has sat in the warehouse and on your shelf.

All I can say is that fresh pasta cooks quickly, and that you should start testing it as soon as the water in the pot returns to the boil. Dried American pasta made with all-purpose flour cooks in far less time than the instruction on its box recommends, and should be tested after 3 or 4 minutes: it can become mushy very quickly. And I've had dried durum-wheat pasta from Italy that was supposed to be done in 8 minutes, and that I had to cook for a full 15 minutes before it lost the final core of uncooked dough in the center. I just had to keep fishing out strands with a fork and biting them until the noodles were at the point I wanted.

You start with a big potful of furiously boiling water. Your pot should be really big, holding 8 to 10 quarts. Buy one with high sides so that it sits right over your burner.

I've seen pots that had strainers or steamers that fit right into them, so that when it was time to take out the noodles you simply lifted out the strainer and the excess water ran back into the pot. This is especially good for making lasagne, when you cook only a few strips at a time, and want to save the boiling water.

For stirring, many people like to use *wooden paddles* that look like flattened spoons with 1-inch-long wooden sticks protruding from them. They're pretty good because they don't tear the pasta, but I've always used a big fork and spoon or a set of *tongs* instead. The point of using wood rather than metal is that wood doesn't conduct the heat from the boiling water to your hand.

A *flat skimmer*, like a gigantic tea strainer, is useful for removing the first batch of wontons or kreplach from the water before you drop in the second batch.

And you'll need a big *colander* for draining the pasta. Be sure that you've got one that's large enough, and that it stands steadily on a circular

base and not on three rickety feet. Otherwise, one day you'll pour in the noodles and boiling water and see the colander tip over and dump your noodles down the drain.

As for rinsing, I know that some books tell you to rinse the drained pasta under cold water to get rid of the starch. All that does is cool off your noodles, and I think it's a damned silly idea. Should you rinse with hot tap water? Frankly, I usually don't rinse the noodles at all, letting the volume of boiling water that pours over them from the pot carry away anything that shouldn't be there. But, if they should stick, then go ahead and rinse. Just use very hot water.

One important point: Don't let the pasta sit in the colander while you prepare a sauce—even a quick sauce. Pasta should be tossed as soon as it has drained. After it's drained, the pasta should go into a heated bowl and be mixed immediately with some or all of the sauce. However, if you want the noodles to cool for a salad, then add some butter or oil and toss gently, to keep the strands from sticking together as they cool.

Sometimes it's a good idea to add the noodles to the pot that holds the simmering sauce, give it a good stir, and let it warm over a very low flame for 1 or 2 minutes while you get the warm plates for serving.

Portions

The rule of thumb is that a pound of pasta serves 4 to 6 people as a main course and 6 to 8 people as an appetizer. If you need a rule of thumb, that's as good as any, but it doesn't take into account the richness of the sauce, the level of formality of the meal, or the appetites of your guests.

At a trattoria in Italy you are served a great glob of noodles as a first course, because they aren't going to give you a large portion of meat afterward. But in an elegant restaurant in New York you may get just a heaping soupspoonful of angel hair with truffles as an appetizer, just enough to awaken your palate. And what about a dish like macaroni and cheese? The meat eaters will take small helpings alongside their hamburgers. The vegetarians will serve themselves quite a lot, since it is their main dish. And the dieters won't take any at all, but will pick the best chewy burnt bits off their neighbors' plates.

That's why I've been imprecise when giving the number of servings you will get from the recipes in the book, why I say that a dish will serve "4 to 6" instead of being more definite. The number of servings will depend on the place in the meal, the quality of the sauce, and the appetites of the eaters.

Important Ingredients

TOMATOES

If you can buy good fresh tomatoes that are sweet and juicy and well fleshed, then you are blessed. Unfortunately, there is a terrific variation in the quality of tomatoes on the market, and most often what you get are tomatoes that taste like pink flannel and feel as though they were put up in a munitions factory. You can't judge by the look of them, either. I've often been fooled by beautifully scarlet Italian plum tomatoes that turned out to have no taste at all. Just now, I'm having good luck with tomatoes that are imported from Israel, but who knows how long that will last?

If you can't get wonderful fresh tomatoes, canned tomatoes are your best bet. The large canneries buy up the pick of the crop, and they put them in cans when they are really ripe. You'll have to test a number of different brands to find the one you like best that is sold in your area. Over a period of years I have found that the Redpack tomatoes canned in purée have been reliable, delivering an intense tomato flavor and cooking down well. They're second only to first-rate fresh tomatoes.

But they're not the same as fresh, and I'm afraid that they don't work the same. That means that the result of your cooking may well vary depending on whether you use good fresh tomatoes, bad fresh tomatoes, canned tomatoes, or canned tomatoes in purée. You'll have to adapt your cooking method to the kind of tomatoes you have available.

If you find that your canned tomatoes are watery, you can either cook them down or intensify the flavor by adding tomato paste. I prefer to cook them down, because I think that tomato paste sometimes gives an overly sweet taste with a bitterness just behind it. But, if you do use paste, by all means look for the kind that comes in tubes. That's one of the most sensible innovations in packaging I've seen in years, allowing you not to feel conscience-stricken if you use only one tablespoonful at a time.

And, if you're lucky enough to find a farm stand selling slightly over-the-hill end-of-summer tomatoes, buy all they will sell you. They may not be right for slicing anymore, but they'll be wonderful to peel, seed, and cook with onion and garlic into a huge pot of tomato sauce. Frozen in 1-cup portions, the sauce will brighten your kitchen all winter long.

TO PREPARE FRESH TOMATOES FOR SAUCE:

Dip tomatoes in boiling water for 30 seconds. Remove skin and cut a slice from the stem end. Squeeze tomatoes firmly to extract seeds and liquid. Chop flesh very fine.

OLIVE OIL

Olive oil comes in several grades, of which the top of the line is called "extra-virgin olive oil." This means oil from the first pressing of the olive, and it is rare in this country. The best and fruitiest olive oil, to my mind, comes from the South of France. After that, in descending order, come oils from Italy, Greece, Spain, and North Africa. Lately, we have been given an extremely good olive oil that is produced in the Napa Valley in California.

Don't store olive oil in the refrigerator, or it will thicken and turn cloudy. Instead, leave it out on the pantry shelf. When kept too long or exposed to heat, olive oil can turn rancid, so it is best to buy it in small quantities if you don't use a great deal.

When the flavor of olive oil is not part of the essential taste of a dish, I often use a good cooking oil, such as peanut oil, or I mix peanut and olive oils half and half, to temper the taste of the olive so that it doesn't overwhelm the other ingredients.

CHEESE

If I had written this book twenty-five years ago, I would have limited the cheeses to Parmesan, Romano, Cheddar, cottage, and Swiss. Perhaps I would have mentioned mozzarella, too, but I'm not sure. In that short list I would have named every cheese I could be sure was available to my readers.

Since that time, however, there has been a revolution in the kinds of cheese we enjoy and import. (And those terms are not at all synonymous: I have no patience with the kind of snob who says there are no American cheeses worth eating!) Our palates have become accustomed to a great many new cheese flavors. And every season brings several new names to our local cheese shops: new varieties of cheese, variations on old favorites, familiar types of cheese now being made in new locations. Twenty-five years ago, goat cheese was considered too chalky and sharp for the American market. Then we learned that goats' milk is naturally low in fat. And now Ed Edelman, who runs the Ideal Cheese Shop in Manhattan, tells me that he carries twenty-five different kinds of chèvre at all times.

Best of all, this explosion of interest has been in the realm of natural cheese. It has nothing to do with all the processed cheese and processed cheese food and imitation processed cheese food, all of which taste like rubber and all of which act in an infuriatingly unpredictable manner when you try to cook with them.

When I was testing recipes for *The New James Beard*, I saw that there had been a revolution in our eating habits and our cooking. We are going through an especially lively period in the history of cooking. Rules are being thrown off. Recipes are finally recognized as guides rather than as commandments.

I refuse to accept that any cook be bound by rules and restrictions. Your taste is your only guideline, and the more you follow your taste, the better cook you're going to be. If there is no good melon to serve with your prosciutto, you can have it instead with figs, or with thin slices of melting-ripe pear or with fresh pineapple: whatever is freshest and appeals most to your palate.

The same freedom applies when we cook with cheese. Constantly tasting as he goes, the new cook learns to appreciate the subtle changes that occur when he uses a mild Danish blue cheese, a sharp Roquefort, a creamy Gorgonzola, or a mellow Stilton. If the tomatoes seem flavorless, he selects a strong Italian Fontina rather than a bland mozzarella to melt over them.

The only rule is to taste as you cook, and to do it often. Never let a recipe become a rigid formula. There is no such thing as the right cheese for a particular dish. During the months when I was testing the recipes for homemade noodles for this book, I happened to have on hand a large wedge of pungent caciocavallo, a hard, salty cheese from Italy. At the end of most testing sessions, when the fresh noodles went into the boiling water, a piece of caciocavallo would go into the food processor at the same time, and lunch would be hot noodles, unsalted butter, and tangy grated caciocavallo. But I could just as well have used an aged Gouda or a true Parmesan on the pasta.

There are reasons beyond taste to free yourself from rigid formulas for cooking with cheese. The "right" cheese might not be available to you. In Greenwich Village, where I live, I am surrounded by well-stocked cheese stores, and in my travels around the country to teach I have seldom been in a city that doesn't have at least one—how I detest the name!—"gourmet" shop. Food mail order is a growing business.

Even so, not all dealers carry all kinds of cheese. Stocks fluctuate with the season and with the clientele. And I know, because of the letters I get, that there are many good cooks who have to rely on the supermarket dairy case and who, if they can't get real Parmesan, don't want to be forced to use those dreadful and expensive little jars of pregrated cheese. They're better off using a sharp domestic Cheddar.

And then there is the matter of price. The days are long past when cheese could be considered a budget-priced protein. True Parmesan—the kind that is made near Parma and marked "Reggiano"—is very expensive. Most people prefer to serve it for eating these days, considering it too costly to grate over a highly seasoned sauce. Instead, they will choose another grana from Italy, an aged Monterey jack or a domestic Asiago to go on their spaghetti. It's important to know that there are less-expensive choices available that will in no way diminish the quality of your dish.

While we're talking about price, we should say something about leftover cheese. Many people like to offer a selection of cheese with salad or

fruit at the end of the meal. One thing that destroys me is the way people cut cheese from a cheese board. If you take care of cheese, if you cut it in regular wedges or slices, you'll have less surface to dry out, and you keep the cheese looking good enough to serve a second time. But you can't stand over your guests, glaring at them if they hack off a hunk here and there, and so usually, after the cheese has been brought out two or three times, it turns into a decidedly awkward, mutilated chunk. There's no reason to throw away a piece of cheese just because there's nothing left but an unattractive end. Instead, recycle it for later cooking.

If you have a semisoft cheese, such as an end of Brie or Fontina, slice it with a sharp knife or grate it against the large holes on your grater. If it is a hard cheese, you can dry it out further by leaving it, unwrapped, in the refrigerator for a few days. Then put it in the food processor, grate it, and store it, covered, in the refrigerator or freezer. Most cheese freezes surprisingly well. The next time you need a few tablespoons of cheese to enrich a vegetable soup or a gratin, use the grated cheese.

A word about grating cheese. I like to use my food processor for the job. But Evan Jones, who knows more about cheese than anyone else I know, tells me that in his house they use an old-fashioned four-sided grater. And there are metal rotary graters which many people use, but I find those annoying because I can't put in a big enough chunk of cheese to make it worth the effort and, somehow, it doesn't fit in my hand properly. If you want the cheese to sing with flavor, try to do the grating at the last minute, just as you grind pepper at the last minute.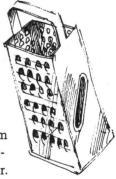

To give you a start, I'm going to list the kinds of cheese we use most often with pasta. I've grouped them according to type so that one can be substituted for another, even though there are subtle variations in flavor. I hope that you will refer to the list before you go to the store, so that you will know what you are getting. Then, if the Gruyère doesn't look good to you, you can select a Danish Samsoe or an American Swiss instead.

I have deliberately left out the soft cheeses such as Brie and Camembert, and the triple crèmes. This is not through any dislike of these magnificent products, but because they are scarcely ever used in conjunction with pasta. But don't let that hold you back if you should find yourself one day with a piece of Boursin and some noodles. Go ahead and put the noodles into a pot of boiling water. Cut the creamy Boursin into small chunks. When the pasta is cooked and drained, toss it with the cheese and a good grinding of pepper. The cheese will melt into the pasta, and you will have a meal for the gods.

HARD CHEESE FOR GRATING

PARMIGIANO-REGGIANO
The prototype: a hard, tangy cheese made from cows' milk in an area near Parma, Italy.

ROMANO
A southern Italian cheese, sharper and saltier and usually less expensive than Parmesan.

ASIAGO
"The poor man's Parmesan," a hard, dry cheese of the grana type, the name given to all cheese of this type in Italy.

CACIOCAVALLO
A white Italian cheese related to kashkaval, and other hard cheeses from the Balkans.

PECORINO ROMANO
Romano made from sheep's milk.

RICOTTA SALATA
A hard, salty cheese made of cows' milk.

AGED PROVOLONE
The familiar sausage-shaped and pear-shaped cheeses that hang from the ceiling in Italian groceries.

AGED GOUDA
Made in Holland of cows' milk, then aged so that it becomes hard and assertive in taste.

SAPSAGO
A very hard green cheese from Switzerland.

KASSERI
An aged cheese from Greece, particularly good in Greek dishes.

AGED MONTEREY JACK
An aged version of the glossy, semisoft cheese from Monterey County, California.

KASHKAVAL
A salty cheese made from sheep's milk in the Balkans and Eastern Mediterranean.

ARGENTINE PARMESAN
Often a good substitute for Parmigiano-Reggiano. Just don't pay top dollar for it.

MOIST, FRESH CHEESE

RICOTTA
A creamy, bland, rather sweet fresh cheese.

COTTAGE CHEESE
A white, unaged cheese made by draining off the whey that forms when cows' milk is heated.

POT CHEESE
A regional name for cottage cheese.

FARMER CHEESE
Cottage cheese that has been drained and pressed, forming a dry, flaky brick.

CREAM CHEESE
A smooth, fresh cheese, usually mixed with carob and gums, but wonderful when unadulterated.

GOAT CHEESE
Fresh goat cheese becomes creamy when melted and adds a distinctive flavor to pasta.

BLUE-VEINED CHEESE

GORGONZOLA
A soft, creamy cheese with a blue-green mold.

DANISH BLUE OR DANABLU
A mild blue-mold cheese made in Denmark with cows' milk.

ROQUEFORT

The only blue-mold cheese made with sheep's milk, made in France, with a sharp and salty taste.

BLUE DE BRESSE

Another French blue, this one of cows' milk.

STILTON

The English blue-mold cheese, rich and creamy.

DOMESTIC BLUES

Such as Iowa Maytag.

SEMISOFT AND NUTTY

EMMENTHAL

The model for all "Swiss cheese": rubbery and mild, with round holes in the loaf.

GRUYÈRE

Smaller holes and a firmer, creamier texture than Emmenthal. From Switzerland.

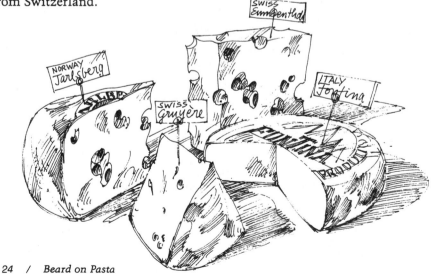

APPENZELLER
Another Swiss-type cheese from Switzerland.

JARLSBERG
Swiss cheese from Norway.

SAMSOE
Danish Swiss cheese.

COMTE
Sometimes called French Gruyère.

AMERICAN SWISS
Whose name explains itself.

ITALIAN FONTINA
A creamy, nutty, whole-fat cheese in a yellow waxy rind.

BUTTERY AND BLAND, FOR MELTING

MOZZARELLA
Originally made of buffalo milk, now of cows' milk. Shiny and sweet-tasting, and a dream to melt.

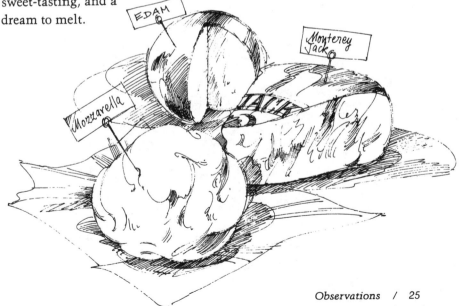

MONTEREY JACK
A glossy semisoft cheese from California.

DOMESTIC MÜNSTER
Very creamy and very, very bland.

EDAM
One of the two famous Holland cheeses: semihard, in a cannonball shape with a red wax coating.

DANISH FONTINA
Made of part-skim milk and covered with a red wax rind.

CREAM HAVARTI
A Danish cows'-milk cheese with a mild, sweet flavor.

TANGY AND CREAMY

CHESHIRE
A cows'-milk cheese from the British Isles, deep orange or white in color.

COLBY
A tangy, firm cows'-milk cheese named for Colby, Wisconsin.

CHEDDARS
From New York, Vermont, Wisconsin, and Canada—excellent in quality,
orange or white in color, also known as rat cheese, store cheese,
or American cheese.

CANTAL
A Cheddar-like cheese from France.

COON CHEESE
A well-aged American Cheddar.

DOUBLE GLOUCESTER
"The golden cheese" from Gloucester, England, whose cows give
especially rich milk.

CAERPHILLY
A crumbly white cheese originally from Wales.

What to Drink with Pasta

You'll want to suit the wine to the sauce. If you're having fettuccine with
butter and cheese, you'll take a glass of white wine with it. But if you're
having a very heavy tomato sauce or a meat sauce, you'll probably prefer a
red wine. A light Italian red wine is just the thing for seafood and tomato
sauces, such as the Linguine with Tomato-Shrimp Sauce or the tuna
variation on page 98.

    With lo mein, Pork with Sauerkraut Noodles (page 142), and curried
beef sauce, nothing would be nicer than lots of cold beer. And with a first-
course serving of pasta with caviar you might want a glass of champagne
or, even better, vodka.

MAKING PASTA

Basic Pasta Recipe
Basic Egg Pasta
(green · tomato · beet ·
golden · basil ·
whole-wheat · buckwheat · Parmesan)
French Noodles
Egg-White Noodles
Barbara Kafka's Buckwheat Noodles
Udon Noodles
Bread Noodles
Bulgarian Shredded Noodles
Spätzle
Spatzen
Nockerli
Potato Gnocchi
(basil and chive · Gruyère and mace ·
tomato and Parmesan)
Gnocchi Verdi

Basic Pasta Recipe

This is the pasta I've been making for years. The recipe makes pale golden noodles with a wheaten taste and a nice resistance to the bite. They are simple enough to enjoy with only a nugget of unsalted butter and some grated cheese, but good enough to be the start of a complicated dish. Once you've learned the basic way, you'll vary the dough according to your imagination, maybe with spinach, maybe with tomato, or maybe beets.

The ingredients are just flour, eggs, and salt. If you mix the dough in the food processor or electric mixer, you will add a tablespoon of oil to the mixture just to get the machine going.

There are several ways to mix the dough and roll it out. By the old-fashioned method—and remember that pasta has been made since the beginning of civilization—the dough is mixed on a wooden board, kneaded by hand, rolled and stretched paper-thin with a long wooden pin, folded, cut, and dried on a rack.

There are people who still swear that this method makes the best noodles. But now that there are so many mechanical aids available to us it would be foolish not to give them a try. I have had many splendid and quick meals of noodles that I made in the food processor and a pasta machine. I can start a tomato sauce cooking on the stove, toss flour, eggs, and oil into the processor, and sit down, well within an hour, to a supper of freshly made linguine with a fiery shrimp and tomato sauce.

I'm going to tell you how to mix pasta dough by hand, in the electric mixer, and in the food processor. Then I'll describe rolling it out with a rolling pin and feeding it through the pasta machine. You will learn to cut noodles with a sharp knife, with a rolling pastry cutter, and with the cutting attachment of the machine. Finally, I will lead you through some of the new machines that promise to mix and extrude noodles all in one process.

My suggestion is that you try all the methods, and then choose the ones that work best for you. One person will enjoy getting his fingertips into the flour and egg, while another prefers the speed and manageability of the food processor. One finds hand rolling a great waste of effort, and another loves the feeling of mastery and control he gets from it. There's no

way to know until you've tried them all. You may waste a dozen eggs along the way but, by the time you're done, you'll be a practiced pasta maker.

If, however, you want to increase your chance of success the first time around, I suggest that you mix the dough in the electric mixer and roll it by machine. Dough that is blended in the mixer falls halfway between ultrastiff handmade dough and the slightly overheated mixture that comes out of the processor. And nothing will build your confidence like watching perfectly cut noodles falling out of the rollers of the pasta machine.

Another way to increase your chance of success is to learn the way pasta dough should feel. Having this recognition in your hands is as important as measuring properly. That's because you will be working with ingredients that change from day to day and from batch to batch. Some flours are drier than others; eggs vary in size; the air in your kitchen ranges from arid to muggy. A dough that works on a dry November day may refuse to roll out on a steamy August afternoon.

But, once your hands know how the dough should feel, it's easy to adapt the recipe to achieve that feeling. If it's too dry, you will sprinkle on some water or add a teaspoon of beaten egg. If it's too damp, you can knead in extra flour. It's not unusual for me to add as much as an eighth of a cup of flour to the amount called for in the recipe.

The ideal, of course, would be to visit an experienced pasta maker and work under his supervision. Some Italians go so far as to say that no one can learn to make pasta who didn't start as a child in his mother's kitchen. But, since that chance is long gone for most of us, we'll have to rely on the trial-and-error method. It just requires some time and imagination.

To get an idea of what you're aiming for, think of the way that perfectly kneaded bread dough feels: plump, smooth, and resilient under your palm. Then imagine a dough that's half again as stiff, and you'll have a pasta dough. It feels moist but not sticky when you poke a finger into it. And, when you knead it, it fights back more than bread dough does.

Basic Egg Pasta

This makes enough pasta to serve 4 as an appetizer or 3 as a main course.

1½ cups all-purpose flour
½ teaspoon salt
2 large eggs
1 tablespoon oil, if using the electric mixer
    or food processor

MIXING

BY HAND

≪ Put the flour mixed with the salt on a wooden board or a counter top. Make a well in the center of the mound, and break the eggs into the well. Beat the eggs with a fork, slowly incorporating the flour from the sides of the well. As you beat the eggs with one hand, your other hand should be shoring up the sides of the mound.

After a while, the paste will begin to clog the tines of the fork.

Clean it off and continue to mix the flour into the egg mixture with your fingertips, just as you would in making any paste. When the flour and egg are all mixed, press the dough into a ball. It will seem to be composed of flakes of dough. Set it aside to rest for a minute while you wash your hands, scrape and clean the board, and dust it with flour. If there are dry flakes that obstinately refuse to become part of the mass, get rid of them now.

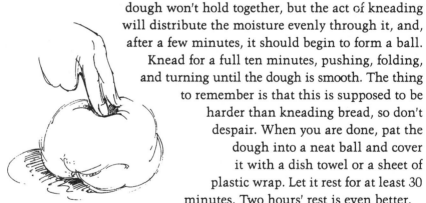

Now begin to knead the dough. Push the heel of your hand down hard, stretching the dough firmly away from you. Fold the flap back toward you and give the lump of dough a quarter-turn. Press down on another section of the dough.

Hand-mixed dough isn't easy to work with. It is stiff-textured and requires a lot of hard pummeling. At first it may seem that the ball of dough won't hold together, but the act of kneading will distribute the moisture evenly through it, and, after a few minutes, it should begin to form a ball. Knead for a full ten minutes, pushing, folding, and turning until the dough is smooth. The thing to remember is that this is supposed to be harder than kneading bread, so don't despair. When you are done, pat the dough into a neat ball and cover it with a dish towel or a sheet of plastic wrap. Let it rest for at least 30 minutes. Two hours' rest is even better.

BY ELECTRIC MIXER

◆੩ Fit the paddle into your electric mixer. Put the flour and salt into the bowl, and give it a quick whirl to mix them. Add the eggs and oil and turn on the beater. Let it go for half a minute, until you have coarse grains of dough in the bowl, something like the consistency of piecrust before it is gathered into a ball.

Replace the paddle with the dough hook and knead in the bowl for 5 minutes. Or take the dough from the bowl, dust a wooden surface with flour, pat the dough into a ball, and knead it for 10 minutes. You will find that this dough is much easier to work with than the hand-mixed dough. After 10 minutes, you should have a firm, smooth, pale yellow ball of dough. Put it to rest under a dish towel or in plastic wrap.

BY FOOD PROCESSOR

Put the metal blade into the food processor. Measure in the flour and salt, and process briefly to blend them. Drop the eggs and oil through the feeding tube, and let the machine run until the dough begins to form a ball; around 15 seconds should do it. Once you've become familiar with the method, you'll be able to correct the recipe at this point. If the dough

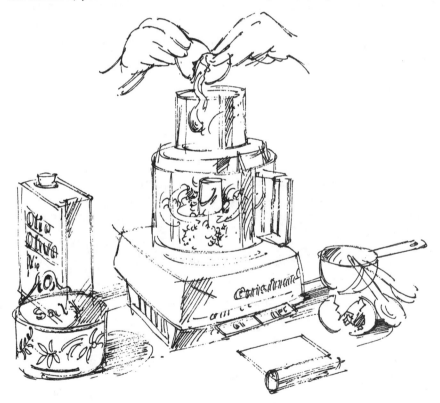

seems too sticky, add a tablespoon or two more flour. If it's too dry, add a few drops of water or part of an egg. Process again briefly.

Turn out the dough onto a floured surface. You will notice that this method results in the yellowest and stickiest dough of all. That's because it's already half-kneaded. Dust your hands with flour and continue the kneading. Work for 3 to 5 minutes, adding more flour if necessary, until you have a smooth ball of dough. Set it to rest under a dish towel or in plastic wrap.

RESTING I

I cannot emphasize too strongly the importance of letting the dough rest between the kneading and the rolling. During this period, which should last at least 30 minutes and can continue in the refrigerator for days, the gluten in the flour relaxes and the dough becomes soft, well blended, and easy to work. I've put many a worrisome dough to rest under a dish towel, only to retrieve it 2 hours later, in perfect condition for rolling.

ROLLING

BY HAND

There are two stages in rolling pasta by hand. In the first, the dough is worked just as it is when you are making piecrust, pressing down and out from the center of the disk. This usually presents no problem for the American cook.

The second stage is harder to learn, because you have to be able to do two things at once. It's a little like learning to pat your head and rub your stomach at the same time: once you get it, it's easy; but the first few times you try to do it, it seems impossible.

To begin, place the ball of dough on a floured

surface. Pat it into a flat disk, and start to roll it with your rolling pin. Move always from the center to the edges of the circle, giving the dough a quarter-turn after each roll to keep the circular shape. Keep checking to be sure that the dough isn't sticking to the board. If it is, loosen with a dough scraper and dust with flour. When the dough is about ¼ inch thick, the first stage is finished.

During the second stage, you will be pulling and stretching the dough instead of rolling it. Very often, I've seen experienced pasta rollers hang one end of the sheet over the edge of the table and lean their tummies against it as they roll. That way, they get a three-way action, pulling, rolling, and stretching!

Curl the far edge of the circle around the center of your rolling pin. Then roll the pin back toward you, wrapping some of the dough around it. Push and stretch it away from you as you unroll the dough. At the same time, slide your hands lightly out and in on the pin, stretching the sheet sideways. Don't press down. Pull out.

Turn the circle slightly after each stretch. You are trying to make a very thin sheet of dough, something like the thickness of good writing paper. It will be slightly transparent. You won't be able to read through it, but if you're rolling on a wooden surface, you should be able to see the grain of wood through the dough.

One way to be sure that you're rolling the dough evenly and that it isn't sticking to the board is to check its color. If the color is more intense at the center of the circle than at the edges, it means that the dough is thicker there. That often happens when it has stuck to the board. Roll it up onto the pin (a dough scraper will be helpful). Dust the board with flour. Turn the dough facedown and flour its top side. Rub some flour onto the rolling pin.

If the business of stretching and pulling and sliding your hands in and out seems too much for you to master, you can roll out the dough as you might a very thin piecrust. It takes a lot of work, because you'll be fighting the gluten's elasticity, but it can definitely be done.

BY MACHINE
There are two kinds of wringer-style pasta machines—one that is turned by hand, and one that is operated by a motor. Each has its advantages and its fans.

The hand-cranked model is considerably cheaper than the motorized machine. And it is my opinion that many people are intimidated by the speed with which the motor-driven machine processes the dough. They like the feeling of being in control that they get from turning the handle themselves.

Other people prefer the speed and efficiency of the motorized machine. They feel that there are never enough hands around to do everything that has to be done with a hand-cranked machine.

All of the machines work on the same principle. The dough is fed through a set of cylindrical rollers, which knead it, flatten it, and, when the rollers have been changed, cut it into noodles.

After the ball of dough has rested for a few hours, cut it into four pieces. Put three of them back under the dish towel, and flatten the fourth with a rolling pin or with your palm. Set the machine so that the rollers are at their widest opening.

If you are using the electric model, turn on the machine (it will make an infernal racket); otherwise start cranking. Feed the flattened ball of dough through the rollers four or five times, folding it in half each time before it goes back through the rollers. This will further knead and smooth the dough.

It may come out with ragged edges or with holes torn in it. This often happens when the dough hasn't been kneaded enough. Don't worry. Patch the holes with bits torn from the end, and feed the dough back through the rollers. If the edges are ragged, fold the ribbon in half lengthwise. If the dough comes out in a distorted shape, just fold it up into a flat square and roll it through again. You'll know when it's rolled enough, because the dough will become smooth and satiny. The nice thing about pasta dough is that it isn't one of those delicate mixtures that shouldn't be overhandled. Go ahead and work with it. It thrives on the human touch.

Now begin to narrow the opening between the rollers by turning the dial one mark each time the dough goes through. Keep going until you reach the thickness you want. Then make a note of the number on the dial, and you'll have something to aim for the next time you roll out pasta.

Lay the ribbon of pasta on a dish towel while you roll out the other three pieces of dough.

RESTING II

Once the dough has been rolled out, it should lie on kitchen towels for around 5 minutes to give it a chance to dry. Machine-rolled dough dries faster than hand-rolled, so the first ribbons will probably be ready to cut by the time the last ones are rolled. Don't let it get too dry, however. The dough should be pliable, neither brittle nor moist and sticky. If it just doesn't dry, dust it with some more flour and no harm will be done.

CUTTING

BY HAND

There are two ways to cut simple noodles by hand. The easier is to fold the dough and cut it into slices with a sharp knife. It's very important that the dough should be well dried if you use this method, or it will stick to itself when it is folded.

Take one edge of the dough and fold it over loosely into a flat roll around 3 inches wide. Continue to fold until the whole strip or circle of dough is folded. Then take a sharp knife or cleaver and cut ¼- to ½-inch slices from the rolled dough. Don't saw. Press down evenly, trying to make the slices even in width. As soon as the whole roll has been cut, open up the noodles so they can dry further.

You can also cut noodles with a rolling pastry cutter. I have one that George Lang gave me that cuts four noodles at a time. Most pastry wheels are single, however, and the problem with using them is that you have to have a very steady hand and a good eye to make the noodles come out even in width.

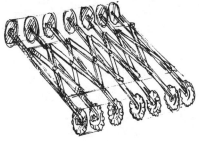

⇜You can use the pasta machine to cut both the hand-rolled and the machine-rolled dough. If you have a circle of hand-rolled dough, just cut the circle into 4½-inch strips that will fit through the machine.

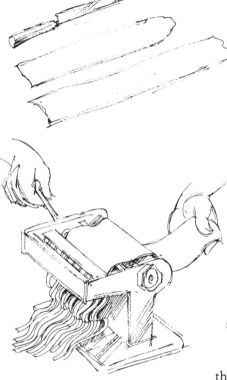

If you are using the electric model, remove the smooth rollers from the machine and fit one of the cutting attachments into place. For the hand-cranked model, insert the handle into one of the cutting slots. Turn on the motor or begin to turn the handle, and feed the ribbons of dough into the right side of the machine. They will come out on the left side in nicely cut strands. If the machine doesn't cut them all the way through, your dough is probably too sticky, and you should set it aside to dry out a little longer.

DRYING

At this point you can simply drop the freshly cut noodles into boiling water. But it is probably more convenient to get the work of making pasta out of the way a little while before mealtime. And many Italians, I ought to mention, feel that drying is an essential step in the making of pasta; that omitting it changes the quality of the noodles. I can't say that I agree, but it is certainly more convenient to make your noodles early in the day and dry them out.

Take up strands of pasta and loop them loosely around your fingers, forming nests. Let them dry on a cloth towel or on a cookie rack.

Or else dry the pasta on a rack. You can use anything—a broomstick, the back of a chair, a clothesline. I've been in Italian kitchens where the fettucine hung like a curtain from a clothesline—strung across the corner of the kitchen. You might want to use one of those two- or three-tiered clothes racks that were designed to stand in the bathtub. I happen to have a marvelous pasta rack that was made for me by a friend. Unfortunately, it isn't available commercially. It's an upright pole with a disk on the top. Three wooden rods fit into holes on the disk. I drape the pasta over the rods. Then, when I want to cook it, I simply pull off one of the rods, carry it to the stove, and push the pasta into the boiling water.

Once the pasta is really dry, you can put it in a tin and store it in the pantry, just as though it were commercial spaghetti. Be careful when you handle it: it will be very brittle. Or you can put the rolled-up nests into plastic bags and stick them in the freezer. But, once you've gone to all the trouble of making it, you will probably just want to cook it.

COOKING

The point to remember about homemade pasta is that it cooks in no time at all. Dried homemade pasta takes a little longer than the truly freshly made, but even so it will be done practically as soon as the water returns to the boil. *Have your sauce ready* before you put the noodles anywhere near the water. And don't pay attention to any recipe that tells you to cook noodles for 8 to 10 minutes. This is too long, even for most commercial brands. (Although I have to say that cooking is the one inexplicable art in pasta making. I find that there is absolutely no way to figure it out when you use commercial pastas. You put it in the pot, and you taste it after 4 minutes, and then after 8 minutes, and finally in desperation after 12 minutes, and it still has the crunch in the middle. I remember cooking some commercial whole-wheat pasta and it seemed that it was never going to become soft.) Have lots of water boiling furiously. I don't add any salt, because I think that your sauce and cheese will provide enough seasoning. But it's a good idea to add a splash of oil to keep the strands from sticking together.

Drop the homemade pasta into the boiling water. Start testing it as soon as it returns to the boil. I've heard all kinds of methods for testing pasta, but the best one is just to fish out a strand and bite into it. If the noodle is beautifully pliable, with no hard core to it, then your pasta is done. Pour the contents of the pot into a colander in the sink, and get ready to mix in your sauce.

VARIATIONS

The same recipe can be used to make different-colored pastas and to incorporate different grains and flavors.

• **Green Pasta**: Add ½ pound fresh spinach, wilted and squeezed dry, or half of a 10-ounce package frozen spinach, defrosted and squeezed dry, to the flour, salt, and olive oil. Use only 1 egg.

• **Tomato Pasta**: Add 2 tablespoons tomato paste to the flour, salt, and olive oil. Use 1½ eggs. Add one to the flour, beat the second in a measuring cup, and pour half of it into the flour mixture.

• **Beet Pasta**: This makes a beautiful scarlet dough. The amount of grated beets you add depends on the richness of color you desire. Start by adding 2 tablespoons grated cooked or canned beets to the basic recipe.

• **Golden Pasta**: This comes from my friend Jim Nassikas, the director of the Stanford Court Hotel in San Francisco. Using the basic recipe, add 7 egg yolks instead of the 2 eggs. If you have trouble making the dough hold together, add an eighth egg yolk.

• **Basil Pasta**: To the basic recipe add 3 tablespoons of a simple Pesto (see page 72).

• **Whole-Wheat Pasta**: I like this whole-wheat pasta. It's very rich tasting. Instead of 1½ cups flour, use 1 cup whole-wheat flour and ¼ cup white flour. Have on hand another ¼ cup white flour to knead in as necessary.

• **Buckwheat Pasta**: Instead of 1½ cups flour, use ¾ cup buckwheat flour and ½ cup white flour. Have on hand another ¼ cup white flour to knead in as necessary.

• **Carl Sontheimer's Parmesan Pasta**: To the basic recipe add 3 ounces grated Parmesan cheese.

French Noodles

Nine egg yolks make this dough so rich that in order to knead it you first have to do a *fraisage*, a special method of blending butter-rich pâte brisée. Once this is done, the noodles are kneaded like any other pasta dough. It makes noodles that are very delicate, although extremely rich in ingredients. I think this is one of the best pastas I have ever tasted.

[6 to 8 servings]

4 cups flour, preferably durum or semolina
1 teaspoon salt
3 eggs
6 egg yolks
2 tablespoons water

◄ Mix the dough as you did in the basic recipe. Make a mound of flour and salt, open a hollow in its center, break in the eggs, yolks, and water, and then combine with a fork until you are forced to continue mixing by hand.

When you have formed the dough into a rough ball and cleaned off the table you begin the *fraisage*. Pull off walnut-sized pieces of dough, and

push them away from you under the heel of your hand, smearing them on the board one at a time. When all the dough has been worked this way, gather the bits back into a ball, using the pastry scraper to help. The *fraisage* will have blended the fat and flour so that the dough can be kneaded. Knead well, and let rest 1 to 2 hours before you roll it out.

This dough keeps very well so if you don't want to use all of it right away, just refrigerate it, wrapped in plastic, and tear off a piece as wanted; it will keep for several days.

Egg-White Noodles

Pasta is actually a low-fat main course, especially when it is served with a simple tomato sauce. But, for those people who can't even take the cholesterol that is contributed by the egg yolks in the noodles, here is a noodle made with no yolks—ergo, no cholesterol—and with one tiny tablespoonful of olive oil.

[6 to 8 servings]

4 cups flour
1 teaspoon salt
1 tablespoon olive oil
7 to 8 egg whites

Put the metal chopping blade in place in the bowl of the food processor. Add the flour, salt, and oil, and process for 8 to 10 seconds. Add the egg whites and process about 15 seconds, until the dough is pliable, but not damp or sticky. Knead by hand for a few minutes, then let rest and roll out by hand or in the pasta machine.

Barbara Kafka's Buckwheat Noodles

This recipe was given me by Barbara Kafka, an imaginative and creative cook. It's different from my own method (see page 45) of making buckwheat noodles because it has no eggs, and because the presence of beer and yeast makes the noodles very light.

[3 or 4 servings]

½ cup beer, at room temperature
1 teaspoon dry yeast
¼ cup buckwheat flour
1 cup white flour
¼ teaspoon coarse salt

In a small bowl, combine half the beer, the yeast, and 2 tablespoons of the buckwheat flour. Stir to make a sponge, cover, and let rise in a warm place for at least an hour.

Stir in the rest of the buckwheat flour, the white flour, salt, and 2 tablespoons of the beer. Use only enough beer to make a soft but firm dough. You will probably not use the whole ½ cup. Cover again, and let the dough rest for 30 minutes.

Divide it into quarters and roll it out by hand or in the pasta machine. Don't hesitate to flour the dough if it seems sticky as you work it. Cut into medium-width noodles.

Udon Noodles

I am indebted to Elizabeth Andoh's Japanese mother-in-law for this recipe. Because the dough is made without eggs or oil, it is very stiff, and the best way to knead it is to wrap it in a few layers of plastic bags and then tread on it. It's great fun to make, and produces thick snow-white noodles that are traditionally used in soup.

[4 servings]

1 tablespoon salt
2/3 cup water
3 cups udon flour*

Add the salt to the water and stir until it is dissolved. Put the flour in a bowl and pour in the salt water. Stir lightly until the mixture is crumbly. Form it into a ball (this will not be easy). Put it in a plastic bag to rest for 30 minutes, or refrigerate for several hours.

Now the fun begins. Put the plastic-wrapped dough into a very sturdy plastic bag. In Mrs. Andoh's book, *At Home with Japanese Cooking*, she recommends stamping on the dough with the whole of your foot. We found that the best method was to tiptoe with the ball of the foot in what seemed a very Japanese manner. When the dough becomes flat, open up the bags

*A combination of unbleached flours available at Oriental groceries, if you can get it.

and fold it into a ball again. Repeat until the dough is smooth and satiny: at least 5 minutes. Finally, stamp the dough into an oval about ¼ inch in thickness.

(If the whole process seems silly to you, you can knead the dough by hand for 10 to 15 minutes if you have the strength, or process it with a dough hook. But I do hope you'll try the stepping technique.)

Roll out the dough on a floured board, stretching it into a large oval. Make 4 or 5 pleated folds, and cut the dough into ¼-inch-wide ribbons with a cleaver or a sharp knife.

Bread Noodles

These are fun, an unusual noodle made of yeast-rising bread dough. It's a good, solid accompaniment to any sauced meat, nice with Irish stew, even better with the Instant Beef Bourguignon you'll find on page 370 of *The New James Beard*. The recipe makes enough dough so that half of it can be used for noodles and the other half for crunchy bread sticks.

[4 servings]

2½ cups flour
½ teaspoon salt
¾ teaspoon dry yeast
1 cup warm water
1 egg white beaten with 1 tablespoon water
   and ½ teaspoon salt
Sesame seeds

In a mixing bowl, blend the flour, salt, yeast, and warm water. Turn out the dough onto a lightly floured board and knead it for 15 minutes. You may have to add extra flour to make a stiff but supple dough. Put it into an oiled mixing bowl, turning so that it is coated with the oil. Cover with plastic wrap and allow to rise in a warm place until it has doubled in bulk, about 1 hour.

Punch down the dough. Return half to the bowl and take the other half to make into bread sticks. With a knife, cut the dough into 8 equal pieces. Using your palms, roll each piece into a thin cylinder about 8 inches long. Cut each one in half and place them, 1 inch apart, on an oiled baking sheet. Let them sit for 20 minutes, until

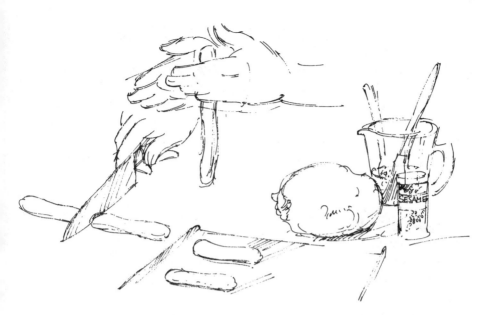

they just begin to soften in contour. Brush with the egg glaze, sprinkle with sesame seeds, and bake for 20 to 25 minutes at 300°. The longer they cook, the crisper they will become.

Meanwhile, punch down the rest of the dough again. Run it through the pasta machine several times, dusting it with flour if it feels sticky. Begin to narrow the opening of the machine and continue until the dough is quite thin. Change the rollers and cut the dough into noodles. Lay them on a wooden board or dish towel to rise slightly while you bring a pot of water to the boil. Drop the noodles into the boiling water. Test for doneness as soon as the water returns to the boil. Drain in a colander and serve with a hearty meat-based sauce and a basket of sesame-studded bread sticks.

Bulgarian Shredded Noodles

This unusual recipe may well be the oldest form of pasta we have. It comes from Bulgaria, but there are noodles like it in modern Hungarian cooking, where they are called *trahana*. I think that these balls of dough were once carried in the saddlebags of nomadic horsemen, then grated into pots of water when they made camp for the night. I make them with a strong, salty caciocavallo cheese that's similar to the Bulgarian kashkaval.

[4 to 6 servings]

> 2 *eggs*
> 1 *teaspoon salt*
> 1¾ *cups flour*
> 1 *cup water*
> 1 *cup milk*
> 2 *tablespoons butter*
> 1 *cup loosely packed grated cheese*

◄⒧Beat the eggs and ½ teaspoon of the salt in a bowl. Add the flour, mixing with a wooden spoon until it is incorporated. Begin to knead in the bowl, and, when all the flour has been mixed in, turn the dough out onto a flat surface. Knead for 3 to 4 minutes more, until the dough is firm, stiff, and very smooth. Form it into a ball, wrap it in plastic, and freeze. This should take at least half a day, but it can, of course, then remain in the freezer for weeks.

When the ball of dough is frozen hard, cover a large area of your kitchen counter or table with sheets of wax paper. Holding a grater over the paper, shred the dough through its largest holes, moving the grater back and forth so that the shreds don't fall on top of each other. When you're done, scatter and separate the bits of pasta so that they won't stick together. Let the shreds dry out on the paper. Once they're completely dry, you can gather them onto a single sheet of paper and store as you would any pasta.

To cook the shreds: Heat the water, milk, remaining salt, and 1 table-spoon of butter in a saucepan. Bring to a boil and sprinkle in the pasta slowly so that the liquid remains at the boil. Lower the heat and simmer for a few minutes, uncovered, until the pasta is firmly cooked and all the liquid is absorbed. Turn it into a baking dish and dot with the remaining butter. Dry out in a 225° oven for 10 to 15 minutes. Just before serving, toss it with lots of grated cheese.

Spätzle

Spätzle are tiny dumplings, bits of dough that are never rolled out but are simply dropped into boiling water, and keep whatever shape they happen into when the water hits them. I've tried two kinds of spätzle makers. One looks rather like a food mill: a circular metal bowl with a flat perforated base and a blade that goes around and around over the base. The other is a rectangular sieve, something like a grater, with a bowl that slides back and forth over it. In both cases, the dough is spooned into the bowl and falls through the large holes on the bottom, being cut off either by the turn of the blade or by the movement over the grater.

But the fact is that you don't need either of these contraptions to make spätzle. I suspect that the original spätzle makers just dropped bits of dough off the tip of a spoon into boiling water or chopped bits off a damp board with a wet knife.

The most elegant spätzle I've ever had was at the Four Seasons Restaurant in New York, where it came with a rabbit paprikash. Use them with beef stew or veal goulash. Or go mad and have them with chili. They'd be wonderful, just the right combination of blandness, starchiness, and chew.

[4 servings]

⅔ cup hard-wheat flour or semolina
1 egg
¼ cup warm water or milk

Measure the flour into a bowl. Add the egg and beat it with a wooden spoon, incorporating the flour. Add the liquid and continue to stir briskly until you have a stiff batter. Put it aside to rest for 15 minutes. It will become even stiffer.

Get your cooking liquid to a rapid boil. If you have a spätzle maker, place it over the boiling liquid, spoon in the batter, and turn the crank or slide the carriage back and forth. Pear-shaped drops of batter will fall into

the liquid, rising to the surface as they cook. Skim them off with a slotted spoon, and put them in a warm bowl with a lump of unsalted butter. If you don't have a spätzle maker, pick up bits of batter on the tip of a teaspoon and flick them off into the boiling water with a second spoon.

Spatzen

I'm not sure why this dish is called *spatzen* and the other is called *spätzle*. I suspect that it depends on what side of the street or what district of Vienna you lived in. The ingredients are slightly different, but the technique remains the same.

[4 servings]

¾ cup flour
Pinch baking powder
Pinch salt
1 egg
⅓ cup water, approximately

Combine the flour, baking powder, and salt in a bowl. Stir in the egg with a wooden spoon, and add enough of the water to make a stiff batter. Set it aside to rest for 15 minutes. Then cook the spatzen by dropping bits of batter into boiling liquid through a spätzle maker or from the tip of a spoon. Drain, mix with unsalted butter, and serve either with gravy or with grated cheese.

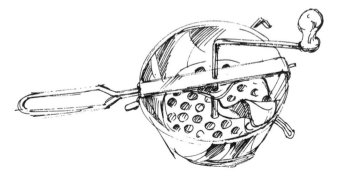

Nockerli

Nockerli are tiny dumplings made by pinching off bits of dough and rolling them into tiny balls. They are nice cooked in a rich beef broth, or mixed with a hearty vegetable, as in the Noodles with Cabbage on page 88.

[8 servings]

2 eggs
3 cups flour
1 teaspoon salt
1 tablespoon butter, melted
¾ cup water

In a large bowl, mix the eggs, flour, and salt. Add the melted butter and water and beat with a wooden spoon for 4 minutes. Let sit for at least 20 minutes. Then, using your lightly floured hands, pinch off bits of dough, roll them gently between your palms, and drop them into boiling water or broth. They are done when they float to the top.

Potato Gnocchi

I love gnocchi. To me, they're sort of magic. They have that soul-satisfying potatoey, floury quality, and with a sauce they are just wonderful.

[6 to 8 servings]

2 pounds potatoes (3 large potatoes)
2 cups flour
2 eggs
2 tablespoons butter
½ teaspoon salt
¾ teaspoon freshly ground black pepper
⅓ cup butter, melted
Grated Parmesan or caciocavallo cheese

Peel and quarter the potatoes. Boil them in salted water until they can be pierced with a fork. Drain, return to the pan, and mash with a fork. Set the pan over a very low flame, and dry out the potatoes, stirring occasionally, until they are no longer gummy. This may take as long as 10 minutes. (You can also bake the potatoes in a 450° oven until they are done, then cut them in half lengthwise and put them back into the turned-off oven to dry for 10 minutes. Remove the insides and mash them with a fork. If you use this method, I need hardly mention, you get to eat all the crisp potato skins.)

Put the mashed potatoes in a mixing bowl and beat in the flour, eggs, butter, salt, and pepper. When all the ingredients are incorporated, turn the dough out onto a work surface and knead it gently for 3 minutes. It will be very soft. Spill a pile of flour onto the work surface, and use it to coat your hands while you work with the gnocchi. Pull off a lump of dough the size of a lemon and roll it into a long sausage as wide as your finger. Work from the center out, trying to make the roll even in width. Continue until you have rolled all the

dough. Then, using a knife or your dough scraper, cut the dough into pieces ¾ inch long. With the back of a knife or fork, make a slight diagonal indentation and fold it in toward the dent. Roll the gnocchi gently under the tines of a fork so that they are ridged.

Bring a large pot of water to the boil. Drop the gnocchi into the water about 8 at a time, and cook them for 3 to 4 minutes, until they float to the top. Remove with a slotted spoon, and arrange in a buttered baking dish. Pour on the melted butter and sprinkle with grated cheese. Heat in a 350° oven for 15 to 20 minutes. If you make the gnocchi early in the day, you can get them ready in the pan and then reheat them for 30 minutes in the oven.

VARIATIONS

• To the basic dough add ⅓ cup chopped fresh basil and ⅓ cup chopped fresh chives.

• To the basic dough add ½ cup grated Gruyère cheese and a large pinch of mace.

• Spread about 2 cups Light Tomato Sauce (page 73) over the cooked gnocchi arranged in the baking dish and sprinkle liberally with Parmesan cheese, then bake as above.

Gnocchi Verdi

These are sometimes called *malfatti*, which means "badly made," because they are so delicate that when they are cooked they are quite uneven in shape. You have to skim them out of the water very, very carefully because of their fragility, but they well repay the care: they just melt on your tongue when you eat them.

[6 servings]

> 12 ounces cooked spinach, drained and
>   chopped (approximately 1 pound fresh
>   spinach, or two 10-ounce packages frozen
>   spinach)
> 1/2 teaspoon salt
> Freshly ground black pepper
> 1/8 teaspoon nutmeg
> 1 tablespoon butter
> 8 ounces ricotta cheese
> 2 eggs
> 1 1/2 ounces Parmesan cheese, grated
> 3 tablespoons flour
>
> SAUCE:
> 1/2 cup butter, melted
> 1/2 cup grated Parmesan cheese

Put the spinach in a saucepan with the salt, pepper, nutmeg, butter, and ricotta. Stir it over low heat for about 5 minutes to dry it out. Remove from the heat and beat in the eggs, 1 1/2 ounces Parmesan, and the flour. Set the mixture aside to cool for 2 hours.

Dust a wooden board and your hands with flour. Pull off walnut-sized pieces of the spinach mixture, and form croquettes the shape of a cork. Roll them in the flour and, when they are all ready, drop them carefully into a large pot of very gently simmering water. Don't let the water boil, or the action may cause the gnocchi to disintegrate. If the mixture seems too soft, don't worry, because the eggs and flour will hold the gnocchi together when they come in contact with the simmering water.

When the gnocchi rise to the surface of the water, they are finished cooking. Skim them off with a slotted spoon, drain them well, and place them in an ovenproof baking dish lightly coated with butter. Pour the melted butter over them, sprinkle with the ½ cup Parmesan cheese, and heat in a 350° oven for 20 to 30 minutes.

PASTAS
IN BROTH

Chinese Noodle Soup
Udon Noodle Soup
Portuguese Fish Stew

Chinese Noodle Soup

My first memory of eating noodles was in a dish much like this one. It also had, as I remember, strips of ham and scallion and delicate bits of egg pancake floating on top, so feel free to add anything you like to the broth. Since that time, by the way, I've always considered noodles one of the standard soup vegetables. Best of all, for this soup, are the fresh Chinese noodles that are sold in Chinatown.

[4 to 6 servings]

6 cups chicken broth, canned or homemade
1 tablespoon soy sauce
¼ teaspoon Tabasco
¼ pound Chinese noodles

Bring the chicken broth to a simmer. Season it with soy sauce and Tabasco. Rinse the noodles and lower them into the pot so that the boiling never stops. When the noodles are cooked, ladle some broth and noodles into each bowl.

VARIATION
• For the egg pancake, smear yolk and white together. Cook on griddle or in skillet, turning once to set. Roll each like a crepe and cut in thin strips to garnish noodles and broth. 1 egg per serving.

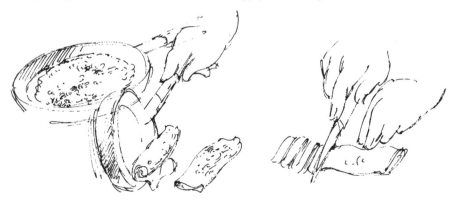

Udon Noodle Soup

The Japanese make a specialty of hearty soups full of thick, slippery udon noodles. Make them yourself, following the recipe on page 50, or buy them in an Oriental grocery. And be sure that the broth is dense with good things to eat.

[4 to 6 servings]

6 cups cold water
1½ pounds chicken necks, wings, and backs
6 slices fresh ginger
2 leeks, washed, including 2 inches of
*   the green*
1½ teaspoons salt
½ teaspoon freshly ground black pepper
2 egg whites, beaten
4 ounces udon noodles
1 bunch radishes, thinly sliced
1 bunch scallions, thinly sliced on the
*   diagonal, including 2 inches of the green*
4 ounces Chinese cabbage, thinly sliced

Put the water in a very large pot with the chicken parts. Add the ginger, leeks, salt, and freshly ground black pepper. Bring the water to a boil over high heat, skim off the froth that rises to the top, and simmer 30 to 45 minutes partially covered.

Line a colander with several layers of cheese-cloth and pour the hot broth through it into a bowl. Discard the chicken bones, skin, meat, and vegetables, wash out your stock-pot, and return the soup to the pot. Bring to a boil and swirl in the beaten egg whites. When the broth returns to the

boil, remove from the heat, and strain it again through a colander lined with cheesecloth.

Cook the noodles in boiling water until they are done. Rinse well, and place them, with the radishes, scallions, and Chinese cabbage, in individual soup bowls. Ladle the hot broth over the vegetables and serve at once.

Portuguese Fish Stew

This is one of my favorite soups, a hearty main-course dish that could be served to friends with bread, cheese, and fruit. It is related to the San Francisco specialty cioppino. I especially like it with orzo, a tiny granular pasta that looks just like rice.

[4 to 6 servings]

28-ounce can Redpack whole tomatoes
   in purée
2 small onions, sliced
5 cloves garlic, chopped
6 leaves fresh basil, or 1 teaspoon dried basil
Salt and freshly ground black pepper
4 tablespoons olive oil
4 cups chicken stock
1 pound peeled cooked shrimp
1 pound fresh tuna, cut in 1/2-inch strips
1 cup orzo

In a very large pot, cook the tomatoes, onions, garlic, basil, salt, and pepper over medium heat for 20 minutes, stirring frequently. Add the oil. Strain or process the sauce and return it to the pot. Add the chicken stock, bring to a boil, and let it simmer for 10 minutes. The soup can be done ahead of time to this point.

When you are ready to serve the soup, bring it back to the boil. Put in the shrimp and the strips of raw tuna, and turn off the heat immediately.

Cook the orzo in boiling water. In the bottoms of 4 to 6 soup bowls, put a large spoonful of cooked orzo. Ladle over the orzo portions of soup containing some shrimp and some fish.

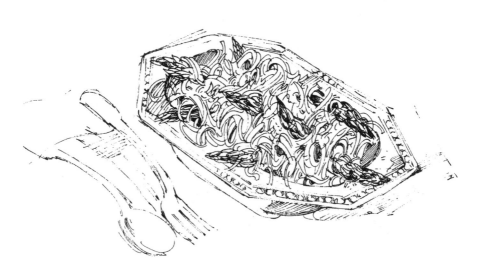

Vegetable Sauces
Pesto
(freezer · with walnuts · with parsley)
Light Tomato Sauce
(with other herbs)
Fresh Tomato Sauce
Mushroom-Tomato Sauce
Spinach-Anchovy Sauce
Braised Onion Sauce
Mushroom Sauce
Herbed Butter Sauce

MAINLY VEGETABLE

Pasta Primavera
Sautéed Vegetables with Spätzle
Spaghettini with Asparagus
Fettuccine with Zucchini
Spaghettini with Fried Eggplant
Pasta Estivi
Mustard Greens with Pignoli
Pasta with Parsley Pesto
Fettuccine with Pesto and Potatoes
Spinach-Mushroom Casserole
Noodles with Cabbage
Vegetable-Noodle Casserole
Pasta with Beans
Avocado Pasta

Vegetable Sauces

I'm beginning the section of vegetable dishes with 8 sauces, all based on herbs or vegetables, to be served over pasta. Most of them are just right for ¾ pound of noodles, that is, for 3 or 4 main-course servings. The pesto recipe makes a great deal more than that, but then in the summer, when fresh basil is available, you should get as much as you can for making pesto and freezing for the winter ahead. The Light Tomato Sauce is another one of those resource sauces that are perfectly good served plain, but that can also be turned into a nearly infinite number of variations.

Pesto

I have basil plants growing in pots in the garden behind my house. I chop the fresh leaves onto summer tomatoes, and every so often I harvest a lot of leaves and make pesto. With pesto in the freezer, I can recover the fragrance of summer in my kitchen all winter long. Use it on plain noodles (you'll need about 1 cup for ½ pound), or to flavor soups, stews, and salad dressings. For an extraordinary treat, combine it with pasta and new potatoes (page 86).

[2 cups]

4 cups basil leaves
3 cloves garlic
½ cup pignoli
½ cup Italian parsley
1 teaspoon salt
½ to 1 cup oil
½ cup pecorino or Parmesan cheese

Put the basil, garlic, pignoli, parsley, and salt into the food processor or blender with ½ cup oil. Process, adding enough additional oil to make a smooth paste. Add the cheese and process a few seconds longer.

VARIATIONS

• **Freezer Pesto**: To make pesto for the freezer: Just process the basil, garlic, parsley, salt, and oil. Freeze it in 1-cup portions. When you are ready to use it, defrost the sauce and put it back into the processor with the nuts and cheese. If you want to use it as a seasoning, you can eliminate the nuts and cheese and simply chip off teaspoonfuls of puréed pesto from the frozen mass.

• **Pesto with Walnuts**: Instead of the pignoli, use ½ cup walnuts and omit the cheese.

• **Pesto with Parsley**: Instead of basil, use 3 cups Italian parsley for a fresh midwinter pesto.

Light Tomato Sauce

I am reprinting this recipe, which was in *The New James Beard*, because it forms the basis for a nearly limitless number of variations. It also has the advantage of using canned tomatoes, so that you aren't dependent on the season or the quality of the tomatoes in your market.

[3 cups, enough for about 1 pound pasta]

*28-ounce can Redpack whole tomatoes
   in purée
2 small onions, sliced
Salt and freshly ground black pepper to taste
1 teaspoon dried basil (optional)
4 tablespoons butter*

Cook the tomatoes, onions, salt, pepper, and basil over medium-high heat for 20 minutes, stirring frequently. If you want a smooth sauce, strain it or purée it in the food processor. I prefer to leave the sauce with lumps, just breaking up the tomatoes with a wooden spoon. Then add the butter and continue to cook until it melts.

VARIATION
• Instead of the basil, substitute 1 teaspoon dried oregano or tarragon or any other herb that you fancy.

Fresh Tomato Sauce

[Enough for 1½ pounds pasta]

4 tablespoons unsalted butter
1 medium onion, sliced
2½ pounds tomatoes, peeled, seeded, and
    chopped (p. 16)
2 teaspoons salt
1 tablespoon fresh basil, or 1 teaspoon dried
    basil, or ½ teaspoon mixed dried herbs
    (optional)
Grated cheese

✥Melt the butter in a heavy saucepan. Add the onion and sauté over medium heat until soft and transparent. Add the tomatoes, salt, and seasoning and simmer gently for 10 minutes. Pour over freshly cooked pasta, mix well, and sprinkle with grated cheese.

Mushroom-Tomato Sauce

[3 cups]

1 recipe Light Tomato Sauce (p. 73), without
   the butter
1/2 pound mushrooms, thinly sliced
4 tablespoons unsalted butter

Cook the tomato sauce. While it simmers, sauté the mushrooms in butter, and add them to the sauce for the final 5 minutes of cooking.

Spinach-Anchovy Sauce

Try this on spaghettini or angel hair to wake up the appetite at the beginning of a meal.

[4 cups, enough for about 1 pound pasta]

1 recipe Light Tomato Sauce (p. 73),
   without the butter
2 tablespoons butter
2 cloves garlic, finely chopped
1 cup chopped cooked spinach
4 anchovies, cut in small pieces
3 tablespoons pignoli, toasted

Cook the tomato sauce. While it simmers, melt the butter and cook the garlic until it is golden brown. Stir in the spinach and anchovies, stir over medium heat for a few minutes, and then add to the tomato sauce.

Toss well, then add the toasted nuts, and serve.

Braised Onion Sauce

Long-cooked onions have a naturally sweet taste. This is a substantial sauce, and I like to serve it with a pasta that has body, something like bows or wagon wheels or wide ribbons or macaroni.

[Enough for ¾ to 1 pound pasta]

½ pound unsalted butter
1½ pounds onions, peeled and sliced
   (about 6 medium onions)
1 tablespoon sugar
¼ cup Madeira
Grated cheese

Melt the butter in a skillet. Add the onions and cook them over medium heat until they are soft and transparent. Stir in the sugar, reduce the heat, and cook very slowly for about 1 hour. Stir in the wine, cook briefly, and pour over a pound of freshly cooked pasta. Sprinkle with grated cheese.

Mushroom Sauce

This makes a nice, quick sauce, even when you use cultivated mushrooms. But if you're fortunate enough to have some wild mushrooms on hand—morels, chanterelles, cèpes, even field mushrooms—you have a great experience in store for you.

[Enough for ½ to ¾ pound pasta]

1 pound mushrooms
¼ pound unsalted butter
3 shallots, minced
Salt and freshly ground black pepper
3 tablespoons chopped parsley

Wipe the mushrooms with a damp cloth and slice them lengthwise, through cap and stem. Melt the butter in a skillet, add the mushrooms and shallots, and sauté them quickly over fairly high heat, tossing them in the pan and seasoning them as they cook with the salt and pepper. Pour over freshly cooked pasta, mix well, and sprinkle with chopped parsley.

Herbed Butter Sauce

I like to make this sauce with tarragon, but if you have a special fondness for some other herb, or if you look on the shelf and there is no tarragon, by all means be flexible. Best of all, of course, is a fresh herb, and I have the idea that more and more cooks are going back to growing their own herb gardens in their kitchen windows or small garden plots.

[1 cup, enough for about ½ pound pasta]

½ pound unsalted butter
1 shallot, finely chopped
1 teaspoon dried tarragon, or 2 tablespoons
   fresh tarragon
2 tablespoons chopped parsley
Few drops lemon juice

Melt the butter in a heavy pan, taking care not to let it brown. Skim off the white froth that rises to the top. Add the shallot and tarragon and sauté gently for about 3 minutes. Add the parsley and lemon juice, stir once, and pour the sauce over hot drained pasta.

Pasta Primavera

In Italian, *primavera* means "spring," and a primavera sauce should be made with the first, tiny vegetables that pop out in the spring. In the winter, of course, you would use the freshest vegetables you could get at that time, such as broccoli, red peppers, and zucchini, but I've suggested a springtime combination that would be just delicious. Just don't be formal about it. Use what you have in the garden or in the refrigerator. You can even cut up a couple of stalks of celery and add them for the bite.

[4 to 6 servings]

½ cup fresh peas
½ cup tiny, new beans
½ cup sliced stalks thin asparagus
½ cup sliced mushrooms
4 tablespoons unsalted butter
1 cup light cream, warmed
Lots of freshly ground black pepper
1 pound angel hair, linguine, or even orzo
Grated Parmesan cheese

Lightly cook the peas, beans, asparagus, and mushrooms in the butter until everything is crisply tender. Add the cream and pepper and cook down briefly. Cook the pasta, drain it, and toss with the sauce. Sprinkle with lots of grated Parmesan cheese.

Sautéed Vegetables with Spätzle

You can use any seasonal vegetables in this sauté, as long as you have an eye for color. This is a good winter combination, with one white, one orange, and one green vegetable. It takes a lot of pepper.

[4 to 6 servings]

1 recipe Spätzle (p. 56)
½ large turnip, in matchsticks
3 carrots, in matchsticks
3 small zucchini, in matchsticks
¼ pound unsalted butter
Salt and lots of freshly ground black pepper
¼ cup chopped parsley

Cook the spätzle. Rinse them under cold water and spread them to dry on a dinner plate. Steam the turnip and carrot strips over boiling water until they are just soft, crisp, and brightly colored. Take them out, plunge them into cold water to stop the cooking, and drain them well. The zucchini do not have to be precooked. All of this preparation can be done several hours before you make the sauté.

When you are ready to cook, melt the butter in a large skillet. Toss the vegetables and spätzle in the hot butter until they are heated through. Do not let them become limp: they should retain their color and stay crisply tender. Season with salt, a great deal of pepper, and the chopped parsley.

Spaghettini with Asparagus

You could try this with any fresh vegetable—peas, for instance, or broccoli—and you'd have an exciting meal. Oddly enough, the Worcestershire sauce doesn't overwhelm the delicate taste of the asparagus. You could use soy sauce, but the Worcestershire gives it a little extra push.

[4 to 6 servings]

1 pound asparagus, cut in thin diagonal strips
4 tablespoons butter
2 large cloves garlic, finely chopped
2 tablespoons lemon juice
1 tablespoon Worcestershire sauce
1 teaspoon freshly ground black pepper
1 pound spaghettini

Heat a pot of water. When it is boiling furiously, drop in the asparagus pieces and cook for just 2 minutes. Pour them into a colander and refresh them under cold water.

Melt the butter in a large skillet. Add the asparagus, garlic, lemon juice, Worcestershire sauce, and pepper. Toss everything well for a minute or two. Cook the spaghettini in boiling water. Drain and then combine with the asparagus.

Fettuccine with Zucchini

A very pretty dish when it is made with yellow eggy noodles, green zucchini, and red pepper strips, like the Italian flag.

[4 to 6 servings]

1 pound small, firm zucchini
2 sweet red peppers, peeled
½ cup olive oil
2 onions, chopped
2 cloves garlic, minced
4 tomatoes, peeled, seeded, and chopped,
*   or one 16-ounce can Redpack tomatoes*
*   in purée*
1 teaspoon salt
⅛ teaspoon dried red peppers, crumbled
1 pound fettuccine

Trim the ends from the zucchini and slice them into julienne strips. Cut the peppers into strips. Heat the olive oil in a skillet, and sauté the onions, garlic, zucchini, and peppers for 5 minutes, stirring occasionally. Add the tomatoes, salt, and dried red peppers, and cook over very low heat for another 5 to 10 minutes.

Cook the fettuccine. Drain and pour the sauce over the hot pasta.

Spaghettini with Fried Eggplant

[4 to 6 servings]

1 medium eggplant
1½ teaspoons salt
Vegetable oil (preferably peanut oil)
½ cup all-purpose flour
1 teaspoon freshly ground black pepper
2 eggs, lightly beaten
2 cups fresh bread crumbs
3 cups Fresh Tomato Sauce (p. 73)
1 pound spaghettini
¾ cup grated Parmesan cheese

Cut the eggplant into ⅛-inch slices. Place in a bowl and sprinkle with 1 teaspoon salt. Weight the eggplant with a plate and a 4-pound weight for 2 to 3 hours, draining off water as it accumulates. Rinse off the salt and dry on paper toweling.

Pour 2 inches of the oil in a deep skillet and heat to 360°. Slice the eggplant across into ½-inch strips. Put the flour and pepper into a plastic bag and add the eggplant slices. Shake well to coat. Remove and dip in egg, then in crumbs, and fry in the hot oil until golden brown. Remove to paper towels.

Heat the tomato sauce. Cook the spaghettini. Drain and pour the sauce over the hot pasta. Serve topped with the fried eggplant and grated cheese.

Pasta Estivi

Some friends brought this recipe back from Italy. *Estivi* means "summer," and it makes an elegant summer lunch, especially good on our basil-flavored noodles. Be sure that the noodles are very hot and the sauce icy-cold.

[2 to 4 servings]

2 large ripe tomatoes, peeled and cut
   into sixths
1 medium onion, peeled and ringed
4 tablespoons olive oil
1 tablespoon white-wine vinegar
Lots of freshly ground black pepper
½ pound green noodles
2 tablespoons chopped fresh basil, if available
Chopped parsley

Mix the tomatoes, onion, olive oil, and vinegar. Sprinkle with lots of pepper, and let sit for at least an hour, to give the onions a chance to lose their sharpness.

Cook the pasta in boiling water, and drain. Spoon the cold sauce over the hot pasta, and sprinkle with fresh basil and parsley.

VARIATION
• Instead of the onion, use 4 sliced scallions.

Mustard Greens with Pignoli

The pungent flavor of mustard greens requires little extra seasoning, but has an irresistible affinity for oil and garlic.

[2 servings]

1 large bunch mustard greens, about 2 pounds
¼ cup olive oil
1 fat clove garlic, peeled
½ pound pasta
½ cup pignoli
¼ teaspoon salt

Wash the greens and chop them coarsely. Heat the oil in a skillet with a clove of garlic, taking care that the garlic doesn't burn. Add the greens, cover the pan, and cook for about 5 minutes, until they are wilted. Shake the pan occasionally to keep them from sticking.

Cook the pasta in boiling water, and drain it. Remove the cover from the greens, add the pignoli, or pine nuts, and remove the garlic clove. Season with salt and pour over the freshly cooked noodles.

Pasta with Parsley Pesto

[4 to 6 servings]

4 to 5 bunches parsley, stems removed
3 large cloves garlic
1 cup whole walnuts
1 cup olive oil
1½ teaspoons salt
¾ cup Parmesan cheese
4 tablespoons unsalted butter
¼ cup chopped dill
   or 1 tablespoon dill weed
1 pound cherry tomatoes
1 pound pasta
2 tablespoons olive oil

Combine the parsley, garlic, walnuts, olive oil, salt, and cheese in the beaker of a food processor. Process the ingredients until you have a well-blended pesto.

Melt the butter in the top of a double boiler over simmering water. Add the chopped dill and the tomatoes. Toss the tomatoes to coat with the dill butter and leave just long enough to heat through.

Cook and then toss the freshly cooked pasta with 2 tablespoons olive oil. Place a portion of the pasta on each plate with some of the pesto on top. Arrange the cherry tomatoes alongside the pasta and spoon some of the dill butter sauce over them. Serve at once.

Fettuccine with Pesto and Potatoes

I first had this at a dreary hotel in Genoa that was tolerable only because the kitchen knew how to do a few brilliant dishes. The tiny waxy new potatoes bathed in basil kept me there long after the beds and plumbing should have driven me away. Try this as a very filling first course, to be followed by some grilled fish or chicken and midsummer tomatoes.

[4 servings]

12 tiny new potatoes; or 6 large new potatoes;
    or 2 large waxy potatoes, enough to make
    1½ cups small potato balls
½ pound fettuccine
1 cup Pesto (p. 72)
¼ cup cream
Grated hard cheese

If you can find really tiny new potatoes, scrub them, leaving the skins on, and boil them until they can be pierced with the point of a knife. If you can't get the tiny potatoes, use 2-inch new potatoes and cut them in quarters, or peel 1 or 2 large waxy-fleshed potatoes, scoop out balls with a melon baller, and cook them until they are tender.

In a large pot of salted water, cook the fettuccine. Drain it and return it to the pot. Add the hot cooked potatoes, the pesto, cream, and some grated cheese.

Spinach-Mushroom Casserole

I made this one night years ago when I was looking for something to serve with a ham that I had braised in Madeira.

[6 to 8 servings]

8 ounces wide noodles
¼ pound butter
3 pounds spinach
½ teaspoon salt
½ teaspoon freshly ground black pepper
¼ teaspoon nutmeg
½ pound mushrooms
1 tablespoon olive oil
2 cloves garlic, finely chopped
¼ cup Madeira
½ cup shredded Gruyère cheese
½ cup grated Parmesan cheese

◄§Cook and drain the noodles. Turn them into a bowl and toss with 6 tablespoons of the butter, which has been cut into pieces. Set aside.

Wash the spinach. Remove the heavy stems and put the leaves into a pan with just the water clinging to the leaves. Cover, and steam the spinach over high heat until it is wilted, around 2 minutes. Turn once or twice with a wooden spoon while it cooks. Drain the spinach and chop it coarsely: you should have about 2 cups when you are done. Season with salt, pepper, and nutmeg, and set aside.

Wipe the mushrooms with a damp cloth and slice them lengthwise, through cap and stem. Melt the remaining 2 tablespoons butter with the olive oil in a skillet. Sauté the mushrooms quickly. Add the garlic and cook for 2 minutes. Pour on the Madeira and cook for 1 minute more.

In a buttered casserole, make a layer of the spinach. Sprinkle it with the Gruyère cheese and arrange the mushrooms on top. Make a layer of the noodles, dot with more butter, and sprinkle with the grated Parmesan. Bake in a 350° oven for about 15 minutes, until the casserole is heated through and a chewy golden crust has formed on the top.

Noodles with Cabbage

I made this up years ago, when I wanted something to serve with sausages and beer. Try it with wide egg noodles or noodle squares or tiny spätzle or nockerli.

[6 to 8 servings]

One 2-to-3-pound cabbage
5 tablespoons butter or bacon fat
2 tablespoons flour
¾ cup light cream
Salt and freshly ground black pepper
1 pound noodles or dumplings

Put the cabbage through the slicing blade of the food processor. Melt the butter or bacon fat in a large skillet and sauté the cabbage until it is lightly browned. Cover and cook for 10 minutes. Sprinkle on the flour and continue to cook, stirring, for a few minutes. Then add the cream, salt, and pepper, and cook, stirring constantly, until the sauce is thickened.

Cook the noodles or dumplings. Drain them, add them to the pot, and let everything bubble together for a few minutes to blend the flavors.

Vegetable-Noodle Casserole

An old-fashioned American dish, despite the tomatoes, zucchini, oregano, and garlic. It was just the thing to take along to a covered-dish supper or to serve to the family for Sunday supper.

[6 to 8 servings]

4 tablespoons butter
2 tablespoons olive oil
3 onions, sliced
1 clove garlic, chopped
1 cup minced parsley
1/4 teaspoon oregano
4 tomatoes, peeled, seeded, and chopped
1 cup chicken broth
Salt and freshly ground black pepper
1 pound wide noodles
3 small, firm zucchini, sliced in rounds
Grated Cheddar or Gruyère cheese

Melt 2 tablespoons of the butter and the oil in a heavy saucepan. Add the onions, garlic, parsley, and oregano, and cook, stirring occasionally, until the onions are golden. Add the tomatoes and chicken broth, salt, and pepper, and cook for 10 minutes.

Cook and drain the noodles. Mix the rest of the butter with the freshly cooked noodles. Stir in the tomato sauce and the zucchini circles and pour the mixture into a buttered baking dish. Sprinkle the top with a handful of grated cheese, dot with more butter, and bake for 15 to 20 minutes at 375°.

Pasta with Beans

This is the heartiest dish imaginable, just the thing for a cold winter night. It's one of those unrefined peasant dishes that deliver a lot of taste, satisfaction, and protein for relatively little cost. Serve with good bread and a simple strong red wine.

[6 to 8 servings]

1 pound dry white beans (pea, navy, or Great
    Northern), or one 16-ounce can white beans
1/4 cup olive oil
1/4 pound bacon, in 1-inch strips
2 onions, chopped
2 carrots, chopped
1 cup minced parsley
1 teaspoon dried oregano
2 tablespoons dried basil
16-ounce can Redpack tomatoes in purée, or
    4 tomatoes, peeled, seeded, and chopped
1/2 cup bean liquid
2 teaspoons salt
1 teaspoon freshly ground black pepper
1 pound elbow macaroni
4 tablespoons butter, at room temperature
1/2 cup grated sharp cheese
Chopped parsley

◄ If you use dried beans, cover them with cold water, bring to a boil, cook 2 minutes, and then remove from the heat and let stand, covered, for 1 hour. If you use canned beans, merely drain them and set them aside, reserving 1/2 cup of the liquid.

Continue cooking the beans over medium heat till they are just tender. Drain. Reserve some of the liquid for the sauce.

Heat the olive oil in a heavy casserole and sauté the bacon strips until they are half cooked. Add the onions, carrots, parsley, oregano, and basil, and cook until the vegetables are wilted. Add the tomatoes, bean liquid, salt, and pepper. Cover and simmer for about 10 minutes, until the vegetables are tender. Add the drained cooked beans and simmer for another 20 minutes.

Meanwhile cook and drain the macaroni. Toss with bits of the butter and grated cheese, and then mix with the bean sauce and a little of the bean liquid. Serve in heated bowls, and sprinkle more cheese and chopped parsley on the top.

Avocado Pasta

This is a superb dish, but it's a bit tricky to handle because of the softness of the dough. You could make only the avocado sauce, and use commercial spinach pasta for the color, but it wouldn't have the delicate sensuous flavor of the real thing.

[6 to 8 servings]

3½ cups flour
¼ teaspoon salt
3 very ripe avocados
3 eggs
2 tablespoons butter
1 clove garlic, minced
½ teaspoon salt
½ teaspoon freshly ground black pepper
2 cups heavy cream
3 tablespoons grated Parmesan cheese
Pimiento

◄§ To make the pasta: Put the flour and ¼ teaspoon salt in a large mixing bowl. In another bowl, mash one of the avocados, which you have first peeled and cut into chunks. Stir in the eggs with a wooden spoon. Add the avocado mixture to the flour and blend thoroughly in the bowl or in the food processor.

Turn out the dough onto a floured board and knead it by hand for 5 minutes. The avocado will have made it very soft, so that you will have to sprinkle it frequently with more flour. Roll it into very thin sheets, using the machine. Cut the sheets into 1½-inch squares. Lay them on a cookie sheet or a piece of foil and chill them in the freezer for about a half hour, until they are firm.

Bring a large pot of salted water to the boil. When the dough squares are firm, take them out of the freezer, drop them into the boiling water, and cook for about 3 minutes, until they are properly done. Drain. Return the noodles to the pot, and add the butter, garlic, salt, pepper, heavy cream, and the remaining 2 avocados, peeled and cubed. Sprinkle with Parmesan cheese and stir gently over medium heat so that everything is coated. Transfer to a serving dish, sprinkle with more cheese, and serve at once, garnished with slivers of red pimiento.

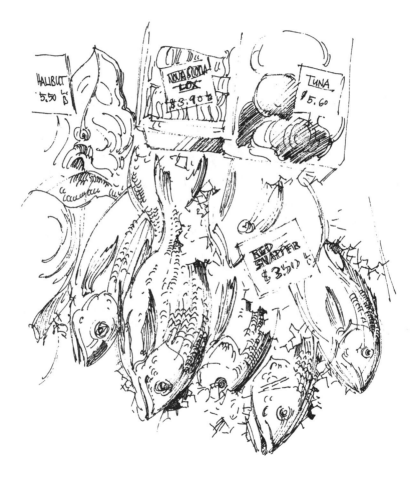

FISH AND SEAFOOD

Angel Hair with Golden Caviar
Spaghetti with Clam Sauce
(with mussels or oysters)
Linguine with Tomato-Shrimp Sauce
(with scallops · tuna · squid · or mussels)
Fettuccine with Striped Bass
(with flounder · with lake perch)
Scallops Provençale over Spaghettini
Swordfish-Olive Pasta
Pasta with Sardines

Angel Hair with Golden Caviar

This is one of the most elegant dishes in the book, and yet it's made in moments. The golden American caviar has tiny eggs, costs far less than other varieties, and can even be stored in the freezer. It's absolutely delicious, and a stunning appetizer.

[4 servings]

1/2 pound angel-hair pasta
3/4 pound unsalted butter, at room temperature
7 ounces golden caviar
4 thin lemon wedges

❧Cook and drain the pasta. Put the freshly cooked noodles into a warmed bowl with the butter. Toss well, until all the noodles are coated with butter, and then put a serving of pasta on each plate. Top each with a heaping tablespoonful of caviar and a lemon wedge. Each person should squeeze lemon juice over the noodles before he mixes in the caviar.

Champagne or iced vodka accompany this admirably. Don't stint on the caviar if possible!

Spaghetti with Clam Sauce

I discovered this wonderfully light sauce, full of the essence of clams and garlic, during one of those periods when I was seriously trying to cut down on oil and salt. I don't think you miss the oil at all.

[4 to 6 servings]

2 quarts little neck clams
White wine
4 to 5 large cloves garlic, minced or crushed
1 pound spaghetti
¾ cup chopped parsley

◄ Scrub the clams well and wash them in cold water to remove the sand in the shells. Put them in a heavy saucepan with ½ inch of white wine or water and the garlic. Cover the kettle tightly, and steam the clams until the shells open, from 5 to 10 minutes.

Cook and drain the pasta. Put the freshly cooked spaghetti in a warm bowl, pour the clams, still in their shells, and broth over it, and sprinkle parsley on the top.

VARIATIONS

• Instead of clams, you can use 2 quarts of mussels or oysters. If you use mussels, scrub them well with a scouring pad, scrape off the encrustations on the shells, and snip off the beards before you steam them.

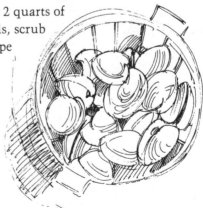

Linguine with Tomato-Shrimp Sauce

Make this mixture as hot as you like by adding a good dash of Tabasco or red-pepper flakes. For me, the hotter the better.

[4 to 6 servings]

1 recipe Light Tomato Sauce (p. 73), without
   the butter
½ pound peeled raw shrimp
2 cloves garlic, finely chopped
3 tablespoons chopped Italian parsley
2 tablespoons olive oil
Tabasco or red-pepper flakes, to taste
1 pound linguine

Cook the sauce. When it is finished, add the shrimp, garlic, parsley, olive oil, and Tabasco or red pepper. Simmer for 3 minutes.

Cook and drain the linguine, and serve with the hot sauce.

VARIATIONS

• Instead of shrimp, use ½ pound bay scallops, or sea scallops cut in quarters; one 7-ounce can tuna; ½ pound squid, sliced into rings; or 18 mussels. If you use the mussels, simmer the sauce, covered, just until the shells open, around 8 to 10 minutes, and keep the pepper seasoning mild.

Fettuccine with Striped Bass

This is a richly flavored, substantial dish that has the springtime flavor of fresh herbs. Most markets have fresh dill year-round these days, but if you want a real treat, make it with chives instead. I'd like to encourage cooks to go back to the old custom of keeping flowerpots of fresh chives growing in their kitchen windows.

[4 to 6 servings]

4 tablespoons butter
1 tablespoon olive oil
½ pound striped-bass fillets,
     or more, if wanted
½ cup cream
Salt and freshly ground black pepper
1 pound fettuccine
½ cup finely chopped dill or chives

◄In a skillet, melt the butter and olive oil. When they are hot, add the bass and cook it on both sides until it is cooked through, about 5 minutes, depending on the thickness of the fish. Flake the fish with a fork right in the butter, then add the cream and let it cook down briefly. Season with salt and pepper.

Cook and drain the pasta. Pour the sauce over the freshly cooked noodles, and scatter lots and lots of dill or chives over the top before you toss everything together.

VARIATIONS
• Fillets of flounder will be a most welcome substitute for the bass. Probably they will be thinner and most likely will cook in less time.
• Small boned lake perch has great flavor and may be used if they are available. Dust them—and I mean, literally, dust them—lightly with flour and cook quickly. Proceed as above.

Scallops Provençale over Spaghettini

Tiny bay scallops should be cooked very briefly, or they become tough, so have everything ready when you make this dish and be prepared to work quickly. The pasta must be cooked before you start to sauté the scallops. It's a nice touch to add a splash of Cognac for quality just at the end.

[4 to 6 servings]

1 pound bay scallops
2 tablespoons flour
1 pound spaghettini
2/3 cup olive oil
3 or 4 cloves garlic, finely chopped
1/2 cup finely chopped parsley
Lots of freshly ground black pepper
2 tablespoons Cognac

Bring the pasta water to a boil.

Toss the scallops in the flour so that they are lightly coated. Drop the pasta into a pot to cook. Quickly heat the oil in a skillet — Teflon is good when you are cooking scallops — and, when it is hot, throw in the scallops and toss like mad. Shake and stir the pan for not more than 2 minutes.

Off heat add the garlic, parsley, and pepper to the scallops and toss for another minute. Pour in the Cognac and cook for another half minute.

Drain the pasta and pour the sauce over it.

Swordfish-Olive Pasta

I like to use twists, shells, or ridged ziti for this dish: something that will catch all the tangy bits of olive and capers. What you want is the rich, exciting olive taste, so use lots and lots of finely chopped Greek olives.

[2 to 4 servings]

½ pound swordfish (1-inch thick)
¾ cup finely chopped Greek olives
¼ cup olive oil
½ cup thinly sliced onion
2 large cloves garlic, finely chopped
1 teaspoon oregano
1 tablespoon capers
½ pound pasta

Preheat the broiler and line the rack with aluminum foil. Broil the swordfish 3 minutes on one side, turn, top with the olives, and broil 4 minutes longer. In the meantime, pour the oil into a sauté pan and cook the onion and garlic until they are soft. Add the oregano and capers.

Cook and drain the pasta.

When the fish is cooked, take it out of the broiler and cut it into thin strips. Spoon it and the olives, with the onion-caper mixture, over freshly cooked pasta and toss gently.

Pasta with Sardines

This recipe is a big hit whenever I teach it in one of my classes. The original called for fresh sardines, but you will probably have to make do with smelts. See if you can get your fish dealer to clean and bone them for you; if not, you'll have to do it yourself. You can use canned sardines, but they are definitely second best. Drain, rinse, and handle them very carefully or they'll flake away to a paste.

[6 to 8 servings]

2 heads fennel
1/4 cup olive oil
1 large onion, chopped
16-ounce can Redpack tomatoes in purée,
    or 5 fresh tomatoes, peeled, seeded,
    and chopped
1/2 cup raisins
1/2 cup pignoli
1/4 teaspoon saffron
1/2 teaspoon dried basil
1 can anchovy fillets, drained, rinsed,
    and chopped
1 pound sardines or smelts, cleaned and
    boned (If you have any tiny fish,
    leave some whole and treat according to
    the directions in the recipe below.)
1 pound pasta, such as penne or macaroni
Salt and freshly ground black pepper

Cut off and discard the fennel tops and cut the bulbs into very thin, lengthwise slices. Cook them in a big pot of boiling water until they are tender, about 5 minutes. Skim them out with a slotted spoon, set them aside, and leave the water at a simmer for when you cook the pasta.

Heat the olive oil in a large skillet and sauté the onion until it is soft. Add the tomatoes, raisins, pignoli, saffron, basil, anchovies, and sardines, and cook for another 10 minutes. If you have any very small smelts, reserve them whole. Drag them through some flour, sauté them in another pan in olive oil until they are brown and crisp, drain them on paper towels, and keep in a warm oven until you are ready to use them.

Turn up the heat under your simmering water. Add the pasta and cook until it is done. Just before you pour it out, return the fennel to the pot to reheat it. Drain the pasta and fennel and pour them into a warmed bowl. Add salt and pepper to taste. Pour on the tomato sauce and mix everything together. If you have whole fried smelts, lay them on top of the sauce.

Penne or Ziti with Tomato–Ground Meat Sauce
(with shrimp · with clams · with mussels)
Verna Ross's Baked Chicken Goulash
and Spaghetti
Old-Fashioned Chicken Fricassee
with Wagon Wheels
Chicken Tetrazzini
(with curry · with truffle and almonds)
Nutted Chicken–Rice Noodle Casserole
Chicken Pot Pie
Coq au Riesling over Noodles
(with guinea hens · with game hens)
Chicken Stir-Fry with Bowknots

MEATS

Pasta-Stuffed Roast Chicken
Pasta and Gizzards
Pasta with Chicken Liver and Artichoke Sauce
Broiled Duck with Rice Noodles
Pastitsio for a Party
Leon Lianides's Leg of Lamb with Orzo
Peking Curry-Tomato Sauce on Noodles
Beef and Scallops
with Cellophane Noodles
Beach Pâté
Chilied Short Ribs over Corn Macaroni
Lasagne
Savory Tongue with Fine Noodles
Ossi Buchi with Orzo
Sausage-Tomato Sauce over Penne
Pork with Sauerkraut Noodles
Soft Noodles Sautéed
Tagliarini Verdi al Guanciale
Gnocchi à la Parisienne

Penne or Ziti with Tomato–Ground Meat Sauce

This is a good scheme to follow whenever you have some leftover meat in the refrigerator. It's delicious made with chicken, beef, pork, veal, even brains. The seasoning will depend on whatever your meat was seasoned with when it was first cooked. If you have some meat juices left from underneath a roast or from a sauté pan, by all means add them to the sauce, too. And, if you don't, and have a delicate meat such as chicken or veal, add ¼ cup cream to the sauce at the end. A wonderful way to use leftovers—let your imagination guide you!

[6 to 8 servings]

1 recipe Light Tomato Sauce (p. 73)
1 cup ground cooked meat
Pan juices or ¼ cup cream (optional)
1 pound penne or ziti

◆ Make the sauce. When it is done, add the ground cooked meat and the pan juices or cream. Season to taste, and simmer for 5 minutes while you cook the pasta. Drain, and serve the sauce over the hot pasta.

VARIATIONS
• Substitute ½ pound or more cooked shrimp for the meat. Add a touch more pepper and ½ cup finely chopped red or green bell peppers.
• Steam clams as described on page 97. Remove from shell and add clam broth and clams to tomato sauce. Combine with pasta. No cheese!
• You may do the same with mussels as with the clams. Remove shell before adding to pasta.

Verna Ross's Baked Chicken Goulash and Spaghetti

This is a very homely dish that I used to eat a great deal in the West. There was a time when everyone was making it. I think of it as very American, one of those things you can carry to a picnic or to a big buffet party. It's quite unsophisticated, but it tastes just fine.

[12 to 14 servings]

4 to 5-pound fowl, cooked and cooled
4 to 5 onions, chopped
4 tablespoons butter
1 pound fresh mushrooms
2 pounds spaghetti
1 can whole-kernel corn, or 1 package
    frozen corn
1 28-ounce can tomatoes
1 package frozen peas
2 cups grated Cheddar or
    Monterey jack cheese

Remove the meat from the chicken and pull it apart into fairly large pieces.

Sauté the onions in the butter until just lightly cooked. Add the mushrooms and sauté a few minutes more.

Meanwhile cook the spaghetti in the broth in which the chicken was cooked. Mix the meat with the drained cooked spaghetti. Add the corn, onions, tomatoes, peas, and mushrooms, and turn the whole mixture into a large casserole. Cover the top with grated cheese, and bake in a 350° oven for 45 minutes.

Old-Fashioned Chicken Fricassee with Wagon Wheels

A wonderfully soothing dish, a great old favorite. If your family likes only the white or only the dark meat, you can buy your chicken in parts instead of whole, and no one will feel disappointed. Wide noodles are traditional, but I served a fricassee with wagon wheels recently, and it made an amusing change.

[6 servings]

4 tablespoons unsalted butter
3½-to-4-pound chicken, cut in pieces
¾ cup sliced celery
½ cup finely chopped onions
2 tablespoons minced shallots
2 tablespoons flour
1½ cups chicken stock
1 cup heavy cream
1 teaspoon salt
Freshly ground black pepper
Pinch of cayenne pepper
⅛ teaspoon nutmeg
2 egg yolks
2 teaspoons fresh lemon juice
1 pound wagon wheels or other pasta

Melt 2 tablespoons of the butter in a large skillet. When the foam subsides, add the chicken to the pan and cook it for 1 minute, until it becomes firm on the outside but has not yet browned. Turn and sear the other side, and remove the chicken from the pan.

Melt the remaining 2 tablespoons butter in the skillet. When it is bubbling, stir in the celery, onions, and shallots. When they are nicely coated with butter, sprinkle on the flour and cook it briefly, stirring all the time. Do not let it brown. Add the chicken stock gradually, whisking constantly to avoid lumps.

Return the chicken to the pan with ½ cup of the cream, salt, pepper, cayenne, and nutmeg. Shake the pan to blend the spices. Bring the sauce to a low simmer, put the cover in place, and lower the heat. Cook over low heat for 20 minutes.

Uncover the skillet and remove the chicken to a covered dish, putting it in a 250° oven to keep it warm. Tip the skillet and, using a flat spoon, skim off the surface fat from the sauce.

In a small bowl, whisk together the remaining ½ cup cream and the egg yolks. Slowly pour about 1 cup of the hot sauce into the egg mixture in a thin stream while you continue to whisk it. Then return the egg-sauce mixture to the pan containing the hot sauce. Cook it over low heat until it thickens to a light, creamy consistency that just coats the spoon. It must not overheat or begin to simmer, or it may curdle. Season with lemon juice and with more salt, if necessary.

Cook the noodles. Drain them, and combine with some of the sauce. Make a bed of noodles on a platter, and lay the chicken pieces on it, coated with the sauce.

Chicken Tetrazzini

Despite its Italian name, this is an all-American dish, probably invented in San Francisco to honor a famous singer. Now we remember her because of this dish. The whole point is in the chicken broth; if you have a good, rich broth, your sauce will be properly flavored. If it's good it's marvelous, if bad—a mess.

[6 to 8 servings]

3½-to-4-pound chicken, cooked
2 sweet red peppers, peeled
6 tablespoons unsalted butter
6 tablespoons flour
2½ cups chicken broth
1 cup heavy cream
Salt and freshly ground black pepper
¼ teaspoon Tabasco
½ cup sherry
1 pound spaghetti
¾ cup bread crumbs
½ cup grated Parmesan cheese

Remove the meat from the chicken and set it aside. Cut the peppers into dice. Make a velouté sauce: Melt the butter in a heavy saucepan, then stir in the flour. When it is cooked and bubbling, stir in the chicken stock gradually, continuing to stir until the sauce is thickened. Add the cream, and season with the salt, pepper, Tabasco, and sherry.

Put the chicken and diced peppers into the sauce, and

hold over low heat while you cook and drain the spaghetti and arrange it in a buttered baking dish. Spoon the chicken and sauce over the spaghetti. Cover the top with the bread crumbs and Parmesan cheese and dot with butter. Place in a 475° oven for a few minutes until the topping is glazed and bubbling.

VARIATIONS

• To make a lightly curried Tetrazzini, add 1 tablespoon or more curry powder to the butter when you first make the velouté. Let it cook for a minute before you add the flour.

• If you are feeling rich and elegant, add a finely chopped black truffle to the chicken. Instead of a mixture of crumbs and cheese sprinkle toasted sliced almonds over the top.

Nutted Chicken–Rice Noodle Casserole

I first had this in a Danish restaurant in Seattle at least forty years ago, and I just loved the crust of buttery, crunchy sliced almonds. I suppose we should offer it to some prima donna, because it's very much like Chicken Tetrazzini. Perhaps, in honor of its origin, we should call it Chicken Nilsson.

[6 servings]

8 ounces rice noodles
3 to 4 tablespoons unsalted butter
3 tablespoons flour
2 cups chicken broth
1/2 cup heavy cream
2 tablespoons Cognac
1½ teaspoons salt; less, if you use canned
   chicken broth
1/2 teaspoon freshly ground black pepper
1 teaspoon tarragon
Dash of Tabasco
3 cups poached chicken, removed from
   the bone
3/4 cup sliced almonds, toasted

Cover the noodles with cold water, and let them soak for 3 to 4 hours. If you use ordinary wheat noodles, cook them in boiling water, drain, and set them aside.

To make the sauce: Melt the butter in a heavy-bottomed pan. Mix the flour into the melted butter and cook it slowly, stirring all the time, for 2 to 3 minutes, until the roux is well blended. Stir in the chicken broth and cook until the sauce is smooth, thick, and at the boiling point. Add the cream, Cognac, salt, pepper, tarragon, and Tabasco, and cook briefly to heat

through and blend
the flavors. An additional tablespoon of
butter swirled in at
this point will give an
even richer sauce. Add
the chicken to the pan,
taste, and correct the
seasoning.

Arrange the
noodles in a buttered
baking dish. Spoon
the chicken mixture
evenly over them,
and cover the chicken
with a good layer of
toasted almonds. Dot
with butter. Bake
in a 350° oven for
20 minutes, when
the top should be brown
and crunchy, an absolutely
delicious finish.

Chicken Pot Pie

Not at all what you think it is. In Pennsylvania Dutch cooking, "pot pies" are noodle squares that are added to rich chicken or beef broth. You serve them in a bowl, with a lot of broth and some of the chicken.

[6 to 8 servings]

4-to-5-pound stewing fowl or roasting chicken
1 leek, washed and trimmed
1 onion, peeled and stuck with 1 clove
1 carrot, scraped
1 clove garlic, peeled
1 bay leaf
2 sprigs parsley
3 peppercorns
Salt

NOODLES:
2½ cups flour
2 eggs
1 tablespoon butter or chicken fat
½ teaspoon salt

Chopped parsley

◄₰Put the chicken in a large pot with the leek, onion, carrot, garlic, bay leaf, parsley, and peppercorns. Barely cover with water (or, for a richer broth, with chicken stock). Bring the liquid slowly to a boil and reduce the heat, skimming off any scum that rises to the surface. Cover the pot and simmer very gently, so that the surface barely moves, for about 1 hour for a young chicken and 2 or more hours for a stewing fowl. Transfer the chicken to a platter and, when it is cool enough to handle, take off the skin, pull the meat from the bones, and cut it into large pieces. Strain the broth, correct the seasoning, and put it back on the stove while you make the pot pies.

To make the noodles: Combine the flour, eggs, butter or chicken fat, and salt with enough water to make a stiff dough—around ½ cup. Make them as you would any noodles—by hand, in the mixer, or in the food processor. Let rest, knead, and let rest again. Roll out the dough on a floured board or through the smooth wheels of the pasta machine. With a knife or pastry wheel, cut the dough into 2-inch squares. Use them immediately or dry them as you would any other noodles.

When you are ready to serve the pot pies, return the chicken pieces to the broth and simmer for a few minutes to heat through. Then lay the noodle squares in the simmering broth and cook them for about 15 minutes. Ladle broth, chicken, and pot pies into soup bowls, and sprinkle with lots of parsley.

Coq au Riesling over Noodles

This Alsatian specialty is a lighter, more delicate version of the Burgundian coq au vin. Any white wine will do, but for authenticity's sake you should try to get a slightly sweet Alsatian Riesling. Noodles, of course, are important in Alsatian cooking, having entered with the German influence.

[6 to 8 servings]

4 tablespoons butter
2 tablespoons oil
Flour
8 chicken drumsticks and thighs
1/4 pound salt pork, diced small
1 pound mushrooms
8 shallots, chopped fine
24 small white onions, peeled
3 carrots, cleaned and cut in rounds
1/2 cup Cognac
Salt and freshly ground black pepper
2 cloves garlic, minced
2 cups white wine
1 pound fine noodles
Chopped parsley

•§Heat the butter and oil in a heavy skillet. Lightly flour the chicken pieces and brown them over medium-high heat, a few at a time, removing them to a large casserole as they are browned. In the fat remaining in the skillet, render the salt pork by cooking it until the fat has melted and the pieces of pork are brown and crisp. Add the mushrooms, shallots, onions, and carrots and toss them in the fat until they are lightly browned. Add them to the chicken pieces in the casserole.

In a small saucepan, heat the Cognac. Pour it over the chicken and vegetables and set it afire. Baste the chicken with the blazing Cognac until the flames have died down, and season with salt, pepper, and garlic. Add the wine and simmer, covered, for 20 minutes. If the sauce seems too thin, thicken it with a beurre manié made of equal parts of butter and flour worked together with a fork and then dropped, bit by bit, into the simmering sauce.

Cook and drain the noodles. Make a bed of the cooked noodles on a heated platter. Arrange the chicken and vegetables on them, spoon on the sauce, and sprinkle everything with chopped parsley.

VARIATIONS

• If they are available in your part of the country, cut up 2 guinea hens. Test for tenderness. Follow the rule for the chicken.

• Several kinds of game hens may be prepared the same way. Game hens should, if they are large, be cut in half. You will need ½ game hen per person. They will cook in approximately the same time after browning in the skillet. Quail will take less time but they are most satisfactory in flavor. Gauge at least 2 per person. Watch them very carefully lest they overcook.

Chicken Stir-Fry with Bowknots

This is a dish that tastes even better when you eat it cold the day after it is served. It's a mad combination of Italian, Chinese, and American foods, and it's just delicious.

[4 servings]

1 large or 2 small chicken breasts, boned
3 Italian sausages
Gizzard, heart, and liver of a
  chicken (optional)
¾ cup olive oil
3 medium onions, chopped
2 carrots, shredded
1 large clove garlic, chopped
2½ cups Light Tomato Sauce (p. 73)
1 teaspoon Oriental 5-spice powder
1 teaspoon salt
1 teaspoon freshly ground black pepper
¼ teaspoon Tabasco
⅔ cup chopped parsley
½ pound bows or butterflies

Cut the chicken breasts into 1-inch cubes. Cover the sausages, and the gizzard, heart, and liver, if you use them, with water, and poach for 5 minutes. Take them out of the water, cut the sausages into ½-inch slices and chop the gizzard, heart, and liver.

Heat the oil in a heavy 12-inch skillet. Add the onions, carrots, and garlic, and stir-fry briskly for 1 minute.

Add the chicken cubes, sausage slices, and chopped innards, and stir-fry for 5 minutes more. Add the tomato sauce, 5-spice powder, salt, pepper, and Tabasco. Blend and simmer for 3 minutes. At the end, mix in the chopped parsley.

Cook and drain the pasta, add the drained pasta to the pan, and toss everything together well.

Pasta-Stuffed Roast Chicken

This is as good a roast chicken as I've ever had, and I am a fanatic about roast chicken. When it's done at a high temperature, the bird stays tender and juicy, while the skin turns beautifully crisp. The stuffing was made with an interesting Italian double-elbow macaroni, but you could use plain elbows, penne, or twists instead.

[4 servings]

6 ounces pasta
2 small bunches scallions, sliced
2/3 cup chopped Italian parsley
2 tablespoons pignoli
1 cup Pesto (p. 72)
4-to-5-pound roasting chicken
2 tablespoons butter
4 slices bacon

Cook and drain the pasta. Combine the pasta, scallions, parsley, pignoli, and pesto in a mixing bowl. Stuff the chicken with the dressing and close the opening by placing a slice of bread over it. Truss the chicken and rub it lightly with the butter.

Place the bird on its side on a rack in a shallow roasting pan. Cover with the bacon slices. Roast for 25 minutes at 425°. Remove the bacon, turn the bird onto its other side, and cover with the same strips of bacon. Roast another 25 minutes. Place the chicken breast up, and discard the bacon. Roast for 20 to 25 minutes longer, basting with the pan juices.

At this point, if the thigh joint moves easily—if you can "shake hands with the bird"—it's too late, the chicken is overcooked and dry! A better test is to insert a meat thermometer into the thigh, avoiding the bone. It should register 160° when the bird is done. Take it out of the oven, place it on a hot platter, and let it sit for a few minutes before you carve it.

Pasta and Gizzards

The lowly innards of a chicken have a wonderful taste and texture when they are cooked properly. This thrifty sauce has the surprisingly Chinese tastes of soy, sesame, and cilantro.

[6 to 8 servings]

1½ pounds chicken gizzards and hearts
1 medium onion, chopped
¼ cup oil
2 large cloves garlic, minced
1 cup scallions, thinly sliced
½ cup chopped cilantro
1 cup chopped parsley
2 tablespoons soy sauce
1 tablespoon Oriental sesame-seed oil
1 pound Chinese noodles

Clean and trim the gizzards and hearts. Parboil them for 30 to 40 minutes, until they are tender, and then cut them into thin slices. Sauté the onion in the oil until it is transparent. Add the gizzards, garlic, and scallions, and sauté them for 20 minutes, stirring occasionally. Season with the cilantro, parsley, soy sauce, and sesame oil, and toss the mixture until it is well mixed and heated through.

Cook and drain the noodles, and serve with the sauce.

Pasta with Chicken Liver and Artichoke Sauce

This rather old-fashioned sauce is lightly thickened with flour. Despite the tomatoes, garlic, olive oil, and oregano, it's not Italian in feeling, and I wouldn't be surprised if it had originated in this country. You might do it with some kind of long, flat noodles, or maybe with twists.

[6 to 8 servings]

4 tablespoons butter
3 onions, chopped
3 tablespoons flour
2 cups chicken broth
16-ounce can Redpack tomatoes in purée
1 teaspoon oregano
2 teaspoons salt
½ teaspoon freshly ground black pepper
¼ cup olive oil
2 cloves garlic, minced
½ pound mushrooms, sliced
8 canned or frozen artichoke hearts
½ pound chicken livers, trimmed
1 pound pasta
½ cup grated cheese

Melt the butter in a saucepan, and cook the onions until they are transparent. Stir in the flour, and cook it gently over medium heat until the roux is golden and bubbling. Add the chicken broth and cook, stirring constantly, until thickened and smooth. Add the tomatoes, oregano, and half the salt and pepper. Cover and cook gently over low heat for 1 hour.

Heat the olive oil in a skillet. Add the garlic, mushrooms, and artichokes, and sauté gently for 5 minutes, stirring frequently. Add the livers, raise the heat, and toss and turn them over high heat until they are well browned. Do not overcook, or they will toughen. Season with the rest of the salt and pepper, and pour into the tomato sauce.

Cook and drain the pasta. Pour the sauce over the freshly cooked noodles, sprinkle with cheese, and serve.

Broiled Duck with Rice Noodles

This is a nice mixture of flavors, but you can use your imagination when you choose vegetables for the stir-fry. I can see putting in some watercress, for example, or some slender new asparagus. The crisply fried rice noodles are fun. People think they have to fry them a long time, but that's not the way to do it. You break them up, drop them in hot fat, and pull them right out. They take one minute, and you keep going until they are all nice and crispy. And excellent they are!

[4 servings]

8 ounces rice noodles
1 large duck or 2 small ducks
1 onion
1 rib celery
2 teaspoons freshly ground black pepper
2 tablespoons soy sauce
Peanut oil
Plum sauce
¼ pound snow peas, sliced on the diagonal
2 bunches scallions, sliced on the diagonal
¼ pound bean sprouts
1 cup sliced celery
2 ounces dried mushrooms, Chinese or
    Italian, soaked and rinsed
2 tablespoons Worcestershire sauce

Soak the rice noodles in cold water for 3 to 4 hours. Remove the breast halves from the duck and set them aside on a broiling rack.

Put the rest of the duck into a pot with the onion, celery rib, 1 teaspoon pepper, and enough water to cover it. Bring to the boil, reduce the heat, and simmer for 1½ hours. Remove the duck from the broth and, when it is cool enough to handle, remove the legs and set them on the broiling rack with the breasts. Skim the fat from the broth, bring it to the boil again, and cook it way down, until it is reduced to 1 cup. Blend in the soy sauce and set it over very low heat.

Brush the duck breast and legs with peanut oil and plum sauce. Place them under a preheated broiler and cook for 5 minutes. The breast meat will be quite rare. You can, of course, cook it longer, but it is tender and delicious cooked just to this point.

Now drain the rice noodles and dry them well on paper towels. Pour oil into a heavy skillet to a depth of 1½ inches, and heat it to 360°. Toss in a third of the noodles and fry for 1 minute. Skim them out, place them on paper towels, and fry the remaining noodles in two batches. Make a bed of crisply browned noodles on a heated platter.

In another skillet, heat 3 tablespoons oil. Toss in the snow peas, scallions, bean sprouts, celery, and mushrooms. Stir-fry over high heat for 2 to 3 minutes. Add the Worcestershire sauce, another teaspoon of pepper, and the reduced duck broth, and toss until everything is blended. Spoon the vegetables over the fried noodles and arrange the sliced duck breasts and legs around the outside of the platter.

Pastitsio for a Party

This is one of the best Greek dishes I know, a good oven dish that's very rich and full flavored. It comes from Leon Lianides, the owner of the Coach House. Patrons of the Coach House know that you can't get Greek dishes there; for that, you have to visit Leon at his home.

[12 servings]

1 cup onion, finely chopped
1 cup plus 3 tablespoons butter
2 cloves garlic
1½ pounds ground lean beef
2 pounds ground lean lamb
Salt and freshly ground black pepper
3 cups tomato sauce
1 teaspoon oregano
½ teaspoon cinnamon
½ teaspoon dried basil
1 bay leaf
½ cup finely chopped parsley
1 cup dry red wine
·7 cups light cream
2 cups milk
1½ cups flour
Good pinch of nutmeg
10 egg yolks
2 cups fresh ricotta cheese
1½ pounds elbow macaroni or ziti
1½ cups grated Romano cheese

◄꜋ First make your meat sauce: In a large skillet, cook the onion in 3 tablespoons butter. When the onion is transparent, add the garlic and cook for 2 minutes. Add the meats and cook over high heat, breaking it up with a wooden spoon until the meat is no longer red. Season with ½ teaspoon salt, 1/2 teaspoon pepper, and the tomato sauce, oregano, cinnamon, basil, bay leaf, parsley, and wine. Cook the sauce, stirring frequently, until most of the liquid has been absorbed. This meat sauce can be prepared in advance and kept in the refrigerator or freezer until you are ready to use it. I never think that far ahead about what I plan to eat, but it's a useful idea if you are making the pastitsio for a party.

To make the cream sauce: Bring 6 cups of the cream just to a boil with the milk. In another saucepan, melt 1 cup butter. Add the flour, stirring with a wire whisk. When the roux is blended and smooth, pour in the hot cream and milk, stirring furiously with the whisk to keep it from lumping. Cook until the sauce is thick and smooth, about 15 minutes. Season with salt, pepper, and nutmeg. Turn off the heat and let the sauce cool for 10 minutes before you add the eggs.

In a bowl, beat the egg yolks with the unheated cup of cream. Gradually add about 2 cups of the warm cream sauce to this egg mixture, beating all the while to make sure that the eggs don't curdle. Then pour the egg mixture into the cream sauce, continuing to stir until everything is blended. Finally, beat in the ricotta.

Butter the inside of a large, deep baking dish. This recipe will need a dish at least 15 by 9 by 4 inches. Cook and drain the macaroni. Place half the macaroni in the dish and sprinkle with half the Romano. Spoon on half the cream sauce, smoothing it with the back of a large spoon. Spread on all of the meat sauce. Now add the rest of the macaroni, the rest of the cream sauce, and the rest of the grated cheese, and place in a 400° oven. Bake for 55 minutes, when the pastitsio should be covered with a golden-brown crust.

If you want to serve it in neatly cut squares, you should finish cooking the pastitsio at least 6 hours before you intend to serve it. Leave it out on the kitchen counter or, if the day is warm, place it in the refrigerator. Then cut the casserole into serving portions and reheat before serving.

Leon Lianides's Leg of Lamb with Orzo

Orzo is a kind of pasta that is ricelike in shape and, almost, in taste. It's an especial favorite with the Greeks and lends itself agreeably to hot dishes, soups, and salads. Use it instead of rice or potatoes as a side dish, with just some butter and a good sprinkle of cheese. You'll find that it won't become gummy as rice may. In this preparation, the orzo soaks up all the wonderfully meaty juices that come from the lamb.

[8 servings]

5-to-8-pound leg of lamb
Juice of 1 lemon
2 cloves garlic
Pinch of oregano
1/2 teaspoon dried basil
1/2 teaspoon dried mint
Salt and freshly ground black pepper
2 onions, coarsely chopped
3-pound-3-ounce can tomatoes,
* about 5¾ cups*
7 cups beef or chicken broth
2 cups orzo
Grated kasseri cheese

◆≷Preheat the oven to 450°. Rub the meat with the lemon juice, garlic cloves, oregano, basil, mint, salt, and pepper. Place it on a rack in a large roasting pan, with the chopped onions underneath. After 20 minutes, turn the heat down to 350°. Add the tomatoes and 2 cups broth to the onions under the pan. Cook the lamb for another 60 minutes, until the outside of the meat is golden brown and the internal temperature registers 135°. The inside will be medium rare, but after it has been kept warm on a heated platter while you cook the orzo, it will be pink and juicy.

Take the lamb off its rack and put it on a heated platter. Scrape all the solids from the bottom of the roasting pan, and pour the juices through a strainer. Return the liquid to the pan with an additional 5 cups meat or chicken broth. Bring to the boil on top of the stove and gradually add the orzo. Stir well, and return the pan to the oven. Cook, stirring now and then, until the orzo is cooked and the liquid is all absorbed. When it's nearly done, carve the meat.

Take the orzo from the oven, turn it into a bowl or onto a serving platter, and sprinkle it with grated kasseri cheese. I've also had orzo cooked this way with cubes of feta cheese mixed through it. Serve some of the orzo alongside the sliced lamb on each plate.

Peking Curry-Tomato Sauce on Noodles

This was a regular offering in Chinese restaurants when I was a boy in Oregon. I never see it on restaurant menus anymore, which is a shame: it has a strong tomato taste lightly flavored with curry. Use it on dried or fresh Chinese noodles or with the Japanese Udon Noodles on page 50. Cellophane noodles are too delicate to stand up to the sauce.

[6 to 8 servings]

½ pound butter
2 onions, peeled and chopped
2 cloves garlic, finely chopped
1 tablespoon curry powder, or more to taste
Two 28-ounce cans plum tomatoes, or
    Redpack tomatoes in purée
1 pound chopped beef
Salt
1 pound Chinese or Japanese
    whole-wheat noodles

Melt the butter in a 3-quart saucepan. Add the onions and garlic and cook them, stirring, until they are soft but not brown. Add the curry powder and cook for a minute to develop the flavor. Then add the canned tomatoes and break them up with a wooden spoon. Reduce the heat, cover loosely, and simmer the sauce until it is thick, around 1½ hours. Break up the chopped meat, drop it into the simmering sauce, and cook very gently, stirring often, for another half hour. Add salt to taste.

Cook the noodles. Drain them, and serve with the sauce.

Beef and Scallops with Cellophane Noodles

This recipe is derived from one that I taught during a series of classes on "Taste" with Barbara Kafka. The beef and scallops make an interesting combination, and are delicate enough in flavor to work with cellophane noodles.

[6 servings]

1 pound cellophane noodles
2 tablespoons oil
1 pound beef tenderloin, in strips 2 inches
*   by ½ inch*
¾ pound sea scallops
1 large clove garlic, minced
1½ cups scallions, sliced diagonally
1 teaspoon salt
Freshly ground black pepper
¼ teaspoon dried red-pepper flakes

🖙 Prepare the cellophane noodles early in the day. Do not soak them. Just break them apart and deep-fry in oil heated to 375° for a few seconds until they puff up. Drain on paper towels.

Heat the oil in a skillet. Add the beef, scallops, and garlic all at once and cook over high heat, stirring, for about 2 minutes. Add the scallions, salt, pepper, and dried red pepper. Cook for another 30 seconds, stirring furiously, and pour over a platter holding the fried cellophane noodles.

Beach Pâté

This is a meat loaf that has tiny pasta shells scattered through it. The shells make a pattern like the bits of tongue or pistachio nuts that are found in pâté de campagne. They're fun, but if you can't find them, try orzo, tubetti, funghini—any small, granular-shaped pasta. I've made this for years and years. It's a perfect dish to take on a picnic and slice on the spot. Hence the name.

[8 servings]

4 ounces very small pasta
1 cup carrots, cut in 1-inch sections
2 medium onions
4 large cloves garlic
½ cup chopped parsley
2 teaspoons thyme
1 teaspoon freshly ground black pepper
2 teaspoons salt
2 pounds beef round, chuck, or rump,
 ground twice
1 pound pork shoulder, ground twice
1 cup fresh bread crumbs
2 eggs, lightly beaten
6 strips bacon

Cook and drain the pasta. Put the carrots, onions, garlic, parsley, thyme, pepper, and salt in the food processor and process for 30 seconds until they are well mixed. Turn this mixture into a large bowl and add the beef, pork, bread crumbs, eggs, and the pasta shells. I like to use my hands for this job, but if you are squeamish, use wooden spoons.

Form the meat mixture into a firm oval loaf.

Make a bed in a shallow baking pan with 3 bacon strips. Place the meat loaf on the bed of bacon, and put the remaining strips across the top. Bake in a 350° oven for 1½ hours, and serve hot or cold. You will find that if you make your meat loaf free-form instead of in a loaf pan, you'll get a firmer texture for slicing and plenty of flavorful outer crust.

Chilied Short Ribs over Corn Macaroni

I've always been a devotee of ribs, no matter how they are done: boiled, braised, or barbecued. I like the combination in this treatment of corn, macaroni, and chili. It should be hot, but not five-alarm hot. If you can find corn macaroni, it makes a good addition to the dish.

[6 servings]

5 pounds lean short ribs
3 large onions, thinly sliced
6 cloves garlic, crushed
4 tablespoons mild chili powder
1 teaspoon cumin
1 tablespoon salt
1 small chili pepper
2 cups tomato sauce
1½ to 2 cups beef stock
1½ teaspoons hot chili powder, or to taste
1½ cups fresh or frozen corn kernels
1 pound elbow macaroni, preferably corn
4 tablespoons butter
½ cup chopped parsley
½ cup grated Monterey jack cheese

◄§ Place the short ribs on their sides in a broiler pan from which the rack has been removed. Broil 6 inches from the heat until the meat is brown. Turn the ribs, and broil until the other side is brown and crisp.

In a casserole, mix the onions, garlic, mild chili powder, cumin, salt, chili pepper, and tomato sauce. Lay the short ribs over the mixture, and pour on enough beef stock to cover. Cover the casserole and place in a 350° oven. After 45 minutes, check to see if more broth is needed. Stir in the hot chili powder and cook for another 45 minutes, or until the meat is tender. Then add the corn kernels.

(If you prepare the ribs and sauce ahead of time, you will be able to chill the casserole and remove the fat that hardens on the top, before you reheat it.)

Cook the macaroni and drain. Toss with the butter, chopped parsley, a few spoonfuls of sauce, and the cheese. Make a bed of the pasta on a serving platter. Arrange the ribs on it, and spoon the rest of the sauce over everything.

Lasagne

Often baked pasta dishes are a bore, but this one holds up, I think, because all the different sauces are first-rate and the final cooking is brief. It looks like a long recipe, but once you have prepared the different elements, you can put it together in a matter of minutes.

[6 to 8 servings]

1 recipe Light Tomato Sauce (p. 73)

MEATBALLS:
½ pound ground chuck
½ pound sausage meat
2 onions, finely chopped
1 small chili pepper, seeds removed
¼ cup chopped parsley
2 teaspoons Pesto (p. 72)
½ teaspoon salt
½ teaspoon freshly ground black pepper
Pinch nutmeg
1 egg

BÉCHAMEL SAUCE:
3 tablespoons butter
4 tablespoons flour
2 cups chicken broth
⅛ teaspoon nutmeg
1 teaspoon salt
½ teaspoon freshly ground
  black pepper
1 cup heavy cream

4 ounces white lasagne
4 ounces whole-wheat lasagne
2 tablespoons peanut or olive oil
2 tablespoons butter
¼ pound Gruyère cheese, grated
¼ pound Parmesan cheese, grated

◄ঃ Make the tomato sauce and set aside.

To make the meatballs: Put everything into a large bowl. Using your hands, blend the ingredients thoroughly and make small balls, around the size of large cherries. Refrigerate until needed.

To make the béchamel sauce: Melt the butter in a heavy saucepan. Stir in the flour, and cook for 2 to 3 minutes, until the mixture is smooth and golden. Remove from the heat while you add the chicken broth, stirring vigorously. Return the pan to the heat and stir with a spatula or wire whisk until the sauce is smooth and thick. Simmer for 3 to 4 minutes. Season with the nutmeg, salt, and pepper. Add the heavy cream, and keep the mixture just below the simmer for a few minutes to blend the flavors.

To assemble the lasagne:
Bring 4 quarts water to the boil.
Cook the lasagne strips, 3 or 4 at a time,
until they are just done. Remove them with a slotted spoon, dip in cold water to stop the cooking, and lay on a dish towel. Continue until all the pasta is cooked.

Melt the 2 tablespoons of oil and of butter in a large heavy skillet. When the fats have blended and are hot, but not smoking, add the meatballs. Cook over medium-high heat, shaking the pan constantly to keep the meatballs in motion, until lightly browned all over. Be sure to keep them hopping in the pan so they do not flatten.

Spoon a thin layer of tomato sauce onto the bottom of a 14-inch baking pan. Make a layer of white pasta over the sauce. Spread on more tomato sauce, and sprinkle with meatballs. Spoon on half the béchamel. Continue with a layer of whole-wheat pasta, tomato sauce, and meatballs and so forth until they are all used up, alternating white and whole-wheat lasagne and ending with the béchamel. Sprinkle with the grated cheeses and bake in a 450° oven for 15 minutes.

Savory Tongue with Fine Noodles

I love the delicate flavor of veal tongue. When I can get them, I will often simmer small tongues in seasoned broth, then let them cool and slice them thin to use in sandwiches, in salads, or in this assertive topping for pasta.

[4 to 6 servings]

1 recipe Light Tomato Sauce (p. 73)
½ cup chopped onion
1 teaspoon salt
Freshly ground black pepper
¼ teaspoon Tabasco
2 cups finely chopped cooked veal or
*   beef tongue*
1 pound spaghettini or angel-hair pasta
Grated Parmesan cheese

Combine the tomato sauce with the chopped onion, seasonings, and tongue in a 2-quart saucepan. Cook gently for 10 minutes.

Cook and drain the pasta. Then spoon the sauce over the cooked noodles and sprinkle with a *great* deal of Parmesan cheese.

Ossi Buchi with Orzo

I've always objected to getting big chunks of ossi buchi on my plate. If you can get your butcher to cut the long bones in pieces only 1 inch thick, you will find that they are still meaty and beautiful, and will cook very quickly.

[4 to 6 servings]

8 to 10 pieces veal shanks, cut in 1-inch pieces
½ cup olive oil
2 teaspoons salt
2 teaspoons freshly ground black pepper
4 cups chicken broth
2 teaspoons basil
1½ cups orzo
Additional chicken broth
2 tablespoons butter
1 teaspoon saffron

GREMOLATA:
4 large cloves garlic, chopped
¾ cup chopped parsley
Zest of 2 lemons

Sear the veal shanks in the oil over moderate heat, turning each piece once or twice. Season with salt and pepper and pour in 1 cup chicken broth. Cover the pot and simmer the meat for 20 minutes. Remove the cover, add the basil, and simmer for another 20 to 25 minutes.

Meanwhile, cook the orzo in the remaining chicken broth. When it is done, drain, reserving ¼ cup broth to soak the saffron a few minutes.

Toss the orzo with the butter and saffron and its broth.

To make the gremolata: Chop the garlic and parsley together with a chef's knife and grate the lemon into the mixture.

Serve the ossi buchi on a bed of orzo, and sprinkle gremolata over the top.

Sausage-Tomato Sauce over Penne

This is a hearty sauce and deserves a substantial pasta, something like penne, the little pointed quills, or ziti, or one of the twists. The seasoning depends on the seasoning of your sausages.

[4 to 6 servings]

1 recipe Light Tomato Sauce (p. 73),
  without the butter
½ pound Italian sausages
1 pound pasta

❧Make the sauce. While it is cooking, cut the sausages into thin slices. Cook them for about 5 minutes in a heavy skillet until the fat has drained out and the meat is cooked through. Pour off most of the fat, and add the meat to the sauce, with a little fat. Simmer together for 5 minutes while you cook and drain the pasta. Serve sauce over pasta.

Pork with Sauerkraut Noodles

An admirable way to use leftover pork loin. If you don't have leftover pork, you can start fresh with thin slices of pork tenderloin, boned pork chops, shoulder, or fresh butt. And, if you use smoked butt, you'll get something else — but something very nice!

[6 servings]

2 tablespoons butter
1 tablespoon oil
2 to 2½ cups thinly sliced cooked pork, or
    1½ to 2 pounds fresh pork
2 tablespoons hot Hungarian paprika
1½ cups white wine
3 cups sauerkraut, rinsed and drained
1 teaspoon caraway seeds
1 pound egg noodles
Salt and freshly ground black pepper
½ cup heavy cream

Heat 2 tablespoons butter with the oil in a heavy skillet. Brown the pork slices on each side over fairly high heat, about 3 minutes to a side. Remove the meat, add the paprika, and cook in the fat for 1 minute. Pour in the wine and bring to a boil, stirring up the flavorful bits on the bottom of the pan. Cook until the wine is reduced slightly, then return the meat to the pan with the drained sauerkraut and caraway seeds. Simmer 10 to 12 minutes.

Cook and drain the noodles. Stir them into the pork-and-sauerkraut mixture and turn gently over medium heat, adding the heavy cream as you do so.

Soft Noodles Sautéed

Because I live so near New York's Chinatown, I can buy fresh Chinese noodles when I make this lo mein. You can do nearly as well with dried Chinese noodles. If you can't find those, thin spaghetti makes an adequate substitute. The trick with this dish, as in most Chinese cooking, is to cook everything very rapidly. You get all the ingredients prepared ahead of time so that the actual cooking takes no more than 5 minutes.

[4 servings]

½ pound Chinese noodles
½ pound roast pork
1 bunch scallions
2 quarter-sized slices fresh ginger
2 cloves garlic
1 pound bean sprouts
2½ tablespoons soy sauce
2½ tablespoons oyster sauce
½ teaspoon salt
3 tablespoons peanut oil
1 tablespoon dry sherry
½ cup chopped cilantro

Cook and drain the noodles. Slice the meat into matchsticks. Cut the scallions into 2-inch pieces and then into lengthwise shreds. Peel the ginger and cut the slices into matchsticks. Peel and mince the garlic. Rinse the bean sprouts in cold water. Pick them over, drain them, and set them aside. Combine the soy sauce, oyster sauce, and salt in a teacup and set aside.

Heat a wok or a large skillet until it is very hot. Pour in the oil. Add the ginger and garlic, the pork shreds and scallions, and stir-fry briskly for a minute. Pour in the sherry, continuing to mix rapidly. Add the bean sprouts while you toss furiously. Pour in the soy-sauce mixture as you stir.

Now add the noodles. Scoop them with the vegetables and meat, running your spatula underneath them, turning them over in the air, and letting them fall back into the fat. Stir-fry over high heat for 3 minutes, until everything is hot and colored with the soy sauce. Sprinkle with the cilantro, give one more stir, and pour into a hot serving dish.

VARIATIONS
• Instead of the pork, you could substitute slivers of chicken breast, flank steak, or tiny shrimp. Instead of some of the bean sprouts you could use thinly sliced Chinese cabbage, pea pods, or bamboo shoots.

Tagliarini Verdi al Guanciale

Where I live, in Greenwich Village, there is no end to wonderful Italian markets, and I have no trouble buying pancetta, the Italian unsmoked bacon. If you can't locate pancetta, you can substitute prosciutto, unsmoked ham, or bacon that has been simmered in water for 10 minutes, drained, and rinsed with fresh cold water.

[6 servings]

8 to 10 medium leeks
6 tablespoons butter
1/2 teaspoon freshly ground black pepper
2 tablespoons chopped Italian parsley
Pinch of nutmeg
Salt
1/2 pound sliced pancetta or American bacon,
*   rinsed and cut into 1/2-inch pieces*
1 1/4 pounds green tagliarini or other pasta
1/2 pint heavy cream
1/2 cup grated Parmesan cheese

Trim off the root ends and most of the green parts of the leeks. Slit the tops and wash thoroughly under running water to remove the grit. Cut into julienne strips and pat dry with paper towels.

Melt 2 tablespoons of the butter in a skillet. Add the leeks, pepper, parsley, nutmeg, and salt. Sauté briskly until the leeks are golden, and remove them from the pan with a slotted spoon. Turn up the heat and sauté the pancetta until it is nearly crisp. Return the leeks to the pan and turn off the heat.

Melt the remaining 4 tablespoons butter in a large saucepan. Cook and drain the pasta and add to the pan. Stir as you add the leeks and pancetta. Blend in the cream and half the cheese, and cook gently for 2 minutes more over very low heat. Serve with the rest of the cheese and freshly ground black pepper on the side.

Gnocchi à la Parisienne

Years ago this was a regular feature on the luncheon menu at the Restaurant Madeleine in Paris. With a green salad, a dry white wine or champagne, and the raspberries to follow, it was sheer luxury. But, if you look closely at the recipe, you'll recognize plain old dumplings, made, this time, with a cream-puff or pâte à choux dough.

[4 servings]

PÂTE À CHOUX DOUGH:
1/2 cup milk
1/2 cup water
1/4 teaspoon salt
1/4 pound butter
1 cup flour
5 eggs

4 large patty shells, or one 9-inch vol-au-vent
7 tablespoons butter
2 cups sliced mushrooms
3 tablespoons flour
2 cups milk, warmed
1/3 cup Madeira
2 cups diced smoked ham
1/2 teaspoon salt
1/4 teaspoon nutmeg
Grated cheese

◄ First make the pâte à choux: Put the milk, water, salt, and butter in a saucepan. Bring mixture to a boil over high heat. As soon as it boils, remove the pan from the heat and begin to add the flour. Beat the mixture with a wooden spoon while you slowly pour the flour into the pan. When all the flour has been added, set the pan back over the heat and beat vigorously for another minute. As part of the water evaporates, the batter will become smooth and pull away from the sides of the pan. Remove the pan from the heat and set it aside to cool for 5 minutes. Make a well in the center of the dough, and beat in the eggs, 1 at a time, beating thoroughly after each addition.

When the eggs are absorbed and the mixture is smooth and glossy, spoon it into a pastry bag that is fitted with a no. 9 plain tube. Have a large pot of salted water at the boil. Twist the pastry bag tightly, forcing the dough to the bottom. Squeeze it out into the water, cutting it off in ¾-inch pieces. If you don't have a pastry bag, you can just take up spoonfuls of dough and push them into the boiling water with a second spoon. Let the gnocchi cook in the boiling water for 2 or 3 minutes. When they rise to the top, skim them off with a slotted spoon and plunge immediately into a bowl of cold water to stop the cooking. Drain and dry on a paper towel.

Put the patty shells or vol-au-vent to warm in a slow oven while you make the filling. Melt 4 tablespoons butter in a saucepan. Add the mushrooms and sauté them quickly. Add the remaining 3 tablespoons butter and the flour and stir them over moderate heat for about 3 minutes. Add the milk and Madeira gradually, stirring all the time, and cook for 5 minutes. Stir in the diced ham and gnocchi and season with salt and nutmeg.

Fill the warmed patty shells with the gnocchi-mushroom-ham mixture. Sprinkle with cheese.

EGGS AND CHEESE

Chèvre-Tomato Spaghetti
(with blue cheese)
Pasta con Quatro Formaggi
Spaghetti Carbonara
(with prosciutto · with pork sausage ·
noodle patties)
Pasta and Cheese Roll in Tomato Sauce
Macaroni and Cheese
Basil Lasagne
Whole-Wheat–Noodle Casserole
Macaroni with Mustard-Cheese
Orzo Soufflé
Angel-Hair Soufflé

Chèvre-Tomato Spaghetti

This combination of tomato and goat cheese is just delicious. Chèvre softens in an especially creamy way; it seems to relax into the sauce. Make the sauce in a pan that's large enough so that you can pour the drained spaghetti into it and let it cook for about 2 minutes, long enough to soak up some of the flavor.

[4 to 6 servings]

1 recipe Light Tomato Sauce (p. 73)
½ cup chèvre, cut in chunks
¼ to ½ teaspoon Tabasco, or to taste
1 pound spaghetti

◄§ When the sauce is finished, add the chunks of cheese to it and let them soften. Season to taste with Tabasco: it should be quite spicy.

Cook and drain the spaghetti. Then add the drained spaghetti to the pan and let it cook for a few minutes more.

VARIATION
• Instead of chèvre, use ¼ cup blue cheese and eliminate the Tabasco.

Pasta con Quatro Formaggi

The only requirement for the four cheeses in this dish is that one of them be Parmesan. Evan Jones, in his *World of Cheese*, makes it with Bel Paese, Fontina, Gorgonzola, and Parmesan. It's not traditional, but I like to use a goat cheese in this dish. It doesn't quite melt; it softens and becomes thick. But by all means go ahead and experiment: this is an excellent opportunity to use up all the leftover cheese in the refrigerator.

[4 to 6 servings]

½ cup butter
1 pound penne or ziti
¼ cup goat cheese, in chunks
½ cup grated Parmesan cheese
½ cup grated Romano cheese
¼ cup shredded Gruyère cheese
Freshly ground black pepper

Melt the butter in a heavy saucepan. Cook and drain the pasta and add to the melted butter. Then mix in the cheeses, one at a time, turning the noodles thoroughly as you go. Serve very hot with lots of freshly ground black pepper.

Spaghetti Carbonara

The trick is not to wind up with scrambled eggs, and that can be managed only if you add the egg mixture to the hot noodles very slowly, tossing them like a demon all the while. Some books specify bacon in a carbonara, and others pancetta. It's not traditional, but I like to use real Smithfield ham, because it tastes better and it never becomes fatty and flabby as bacon does.

[4 to 6 servings]

4 eggs
2 tablespoons heavy cream
Salt and freshly ground black pepper
½ pound baked Smithfield ham,
  cut in slivers
1 pound spaghetti
1 cup mixed grated Parmesan and
  caciocavallo cheeses

In a small bowl, beat the eggs with the cream, salt, pepper, and ham. Cook the spaghetti, and when it is drained return it to the pot over a turned-off burner. Give the egg mixture another stir and then begin to mix it gently and slowly into the spaghetti, keeping it moving all the while so that the eggs don't cook. Add the cheese and continue to toss the noodles until everything is blended. Serve immediately with more grated cheese.

VARIATIONS
• Instead of the Smithfield ham, use ½ pound prosciutto cut in slivers, or ½ pound cooked pork-sausage meat.
• (One of the pleasant aftermaths of Spaghetti Carbonara is a plate of sautéed pasta patties. I can't give proper measurements for this dish because you just use whatever you have left over, but you'll wind up with patties that are crisp and brown on the outside, chewy on the inside, and just delicious with roast pork or broiled chicken.

To make the noodle patties: Melt a stick of butter in a heavy skillet. Then pull off clumps of the cold leftover spaghetti in pieces about the size of a medium cookie. When the butter is nice and hot, place 3 or 4 patties in it. Let them brown on both sides; the eggs and cheese will hold them together as they cook. Take them out of the pan and drain them on paper towels while you make the rest of the patties.)

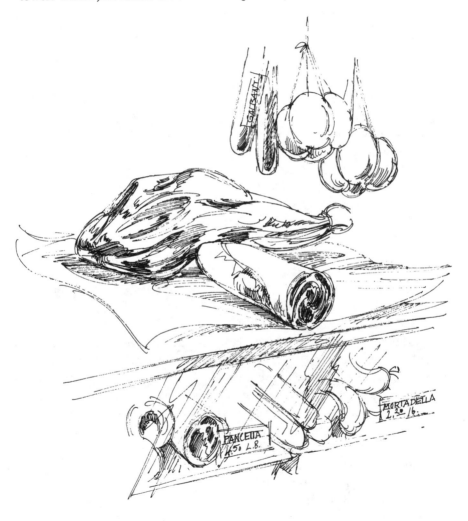

Pasta and Cheese Roll
in Tomato Sauce

This is an amusing variation on a jelly roll. I love the tiny acini di pepe, which look like peppercorns, but you could use any other really small pasta. Try pastina, or orzo, or star-shaped stellini. They have to be light enough so that they don't drag down the soufflé mixture.

[4 to 6 servings]

> 3/4 cup acini di pepe
> 6 eggs, separated
> 1/4 cup butter, melted
> 1 teaspoon oregano
> 1/4 teaspoon thyme
> Salt and freshly ground black pepper
> 6 tablespoons grated Parmesan cheese
> 1 1/2 cups shredded mozzarella cheese
> 1 1/2 cups Light Tomato Sauce (p. 73)

◄Butter a 15 by 11-inch jelly-roll pan. Line the pan with parchment or aluminum foil, leaving an overhang of about 2 inches at each end. Butter the paper well to prevent the eggs from sticking.

Cook and drain the pasta.

Beat the egg yolks until they are light and lemon-colored, then gradually stir in the pasta, butter, oregano, thyme, salt, pepper, and 2 tablespoons of the Parmesan cheese. In another bowl, beat the egg whites until they hold soft, unwavering peaks. Fold the whites into the yolk mixture quite thoroughly. Spread the mixture in the prepared pan, smoothing it with a knife or a rubber spatula so that it is the same thickness overall. Sprinkle it evenly with mozzarella and bake it in a 375° oven for 15 minutes, until it is firm and puffy. Take it out of the oven and turn the oven temperature down to 325°.

With most soufflé-roll mixtures, you would now quickly invert the pan onto a towel and peel off the paper. But you want to keep the mozzarella on the inside of the roll; so, instead, you grasp the extended ends of the parchment paper or foil, lift it out of the pan, and lay it on a large cooling rack.

Let it cool for 10 minutes, and then use the paper to help roll it up, starting with one long side. As you roll, peel off the paper. You may have to use a small, sharp knife to help you along.

Slice the roll into 10 rounds. Arrange them in an overlapping row in a buttered baking dish. Cover them with tomato sauce, sprinkle with the remaining Parmesan, and heat at 325° for 20 minutes, until the cheese is melted.

Macaroni and Cheese

This is a great American classic, one of our best dishes. It has to be gooey, made with a really rich béchamel and with a Cheddar that sings with flavor. I love it when the cheese on top gets burnt and chewy, and I love to scrape up the dried bits that stick to the pan.

[4 to 6 servings]

4 tablespoons butter
4 tablespoons flour
2 cups milk
Dash of freshly ground black pepper
½ teaspoon Tabasco, or more to taste
½ cup heavy cream or crème fraîche
½ pound macaroni elbows or double-elbows
¾ pound grated Cheddar cheese

Melt the butter in a saucepan over low heat. Add the flour, and stir it with a wooden spoon or spatula for around 3 minutes, until the roux is frothy and the taste of raw flour is gone. Meanwhile, heat the milk in another pan. Add the warm milk gradually to the roux, stirring hard all the while. Turn up the heat and cook, stirring, until the sauce is just at the boiling point. Turn down the heat and let it simmer for a few minutes. Now add the pepper and Tabasco. Don't be afraid of the Tabasco: it will help to bring out the taste of the cheese. Stir in the heavy cream or crème fraîche and simmer a little longer, until the flavors are blended.

Cook and drain the macaroni.

Mix three-quarters of the grated cheese into the simmering sauce. As soon as it melts, combine it with the drained macaroni, and pour it into a baking pan. Sprinkle the top with the remaining cheese, and bake for 20 to 30 minutes in a 350° oven.

Basil Lasagne

A thin and elegant version of lasagne, just two layers of noodles with basil-flavored ricotta in between. Serve it at lunch, with a cool white wine and a green salad.

[3 or 4 servings]

½ pound lasagne noodles
½ cup Pesto (p. 72)
1 cup ricotta cheese
1 egg
½ cup grated Parmesan cheese
½ pound mozzarella cheese, shredded

Put the lasagne into a large pot of boiling water.

Meanwhile, using a wooden spoon or the food processor, beat the pesto, ricotta, egg, and Parmesan cheese until they are well blended. Butter a shallow baking dish. Drain the lasagne when just done al dente and make a layer of it in the baking dish. Cover it with the ricotta-pesto mixture and then with a second layer of lasagne. Over this, spread all the mozzarella and sprinkle with more Parmesan cheese. Bake in a 350° oven for 25 minutes.

Whole-Wheat–Noodle Casserole

I love the texture of whole-wheat noodles. They seem to have so much character. This is a good oven dish, a different way to have a starch dish with steak, sausages, or fried chicken.

[6 servings]

1 pound whole-wheat noodles
1½ cups cottage cheese
1 cup yogurt
1 tablespoon Dijon mustard
1 teaspoon freshly ground black pepper
1 tablespoon Worcestershire sauce
¼ pound Gruyère or
    Cheddar cheese, shredded

Cook and drain the noodles.

Combine the noodles, cottage cheese, yogurt, mustard, pepper, and Worcestershire sauce. Turn the noodles into a buttered baking dish and sprinkle the shredded cheese over the top. Bake in a 350° oven for 30 minutes.

Macaroni with Mustard-Cheese

This is a natural to serve at a barbecue with hamburgers or hot dogs. The mustard adds a wonderful tang, and if you're watching your weight, you can simply use low-fat cottage cheese.

[6 to 8 servings]

1 pound macaroni
2 cups cottage cheese
2 tablespoons Dijon mustard
1 teaspoon freshly ground black pepper

Cook and drain the macaroni.

Combine it with the other ingredients and toss well. Although part of the appeal is in the contrast between the hot noodles and cold cheese, this dish can also be mixed ahead of time and served cold or, rather, at room temperature.

Orzo Soufflé

The secret of this soufflé is the egg! The yolks and their treatment are all-important. It is made without the usual béchamel base, so that you have to beat the egg whites until they form soft peaks, and then fold them into the rest of the mixture so that they stay full of air. Then relax and let your soufflé do its thing. Serve as soon as it comes out of the oven, making sure that everybody gets a big piece of the browned crust as well as some of the creamy center.

[4 servings]

6 egg yolks
1½ cups cooked orzo, drained
1 cup grated Parmesan cheese, or ¾ cup
  grated Gruyère cheese, or ½ cup grated
  Cheddar cheese
¼ teaspoon salt
½ teaspoon freshly ground black pepper
Several dashes Tabasco
8 egg whites

✑Put the egg yolks in the bowl of a mixer and beat them until they are thick and lemon-colored, as long as 5 minutes. Beating the eggs very well allows you to make the soufflé without a flour thickening. Add the orzo, the grated cheese, salt, pepper, and Tabasco.

In another bowl, preferably copper, beat the egg whites with a wire whisk or an electric mixer. Beat until they are stiff but not dry. Do not overbeat until they stand upright as though you were making meringues. Stir a large spoonful of white into the yolk mixture. Then fold in the rest of the whites, cutting lightly through the center of the mixture with the side of the spatula, pulling it up and over and then cutting down again.

Pour into a buttered 2-quart soufflé dish and smooth the top with the spatula. Draw a circle with your finger on top of the mixture about 2 inches in from the rim. This will make the soufflé form a cap that rises higher than the rim. Bake in a preheated 375° oven for about 25 minutes, and serve immediately.

Angel-Hair Soufflé

When the soufflé rises, it lifts the very thin strands of pasta and bits of prosciutto with it. Use your imagination when you pick the cheese. I've suggested Cheddar, Gruyère, or Parmesan, all of which have good character and melting qualities. But you might want to try a fresh mozzarella or delicate Fontina instead.

[4 servings]

4 ounces angel-hair pasta
6 egg yolks
¾ cup shredded Cheddar, Parmesan,
   or Gruyère cheese
¾ cup finely diced prosciutto
½ teaspoon freshly ground black pepper
⅛ teaspoon Tabasco
8 egg whites

◄ Cook and drain the pasta.

Put the egg yolks in the bowl of your mixer and beat them until they are thick and butter-colored, as long as 5 minutes. Stir in the cheese, prosciutto, pepper, Tabasco, and the cooked pasta.

In another bowl, beat the egg whites until they form soft peaks that just bend over. Stir a large spoonful of the white into the yolk mixture, and then fold in the rest of the beaten whites gently but thoroughly, using a rubber spatula.

Pour the mixture into a buttered 2-quart soufflé dish and smooth the top with the spatula. Draw a circle with your finger on top of the soufflé about 2 inches in from the rim. This will make the center rise higher than the sides to form a cap. Bake in the center of a preheated 375° oven for 15 to 20 minutes.

STUFFED PASTAS

Stuffed Shells
(with Italian sausage ·
vinaigrette · other stuffings)
Spinach Ravioli
Ravioli with Sweetbread Stuffing
Crabmeat Ravioli
(with tuna · shrimp · scallops
or shad roe)
Stuffed Ziti
Kreplach
Wontons
Tortellini
Frogs' Legs Tortelloni
Steamed Meat Packets
Noodle-Eggplant Dumplings

Stuffed Shells

This is one of those clean-out-the-refrigerator recipes. It is absolutely delicious when made with cooked chicken. But it can be made as well with leftover beef, ham, or veal, and is a wonderful solution for the very last scraps of the Thanksgiving turkey.

[6 to 8 servings]

Meat from 2 chicken legs and thighs, or 1½
   to 2 cups any leftover meat
½ pound mushrooms
3 large cloves garlic
6 sprigs parsley
2 teaspoons dried tarragon
1 egg
1 teaspoon salt
1 teaspoon freshly ground black pepper
½ teaspoon Tabasco
1 tablespoon lemon juice
Thirty 2-inch macaroni shells
2 cups grated Gruyère cheese
1 recipe Light Tomato Sauce (p. 73)

◄ Combine the meat, mushrooms, garlic, parsley, tarragon, egg, salt, pepper, Tabasco, and lemon juice in the bowl of the food processor and process until mixture is well blended.

Cook and drain the shells, and spoon some of the filling into each of the cooked shells. Lay them in a buttered baking dish, open sides up. Sprinkle with most of the cheese, cover with tomato sauce, and then with the rest of the cheese. Bake in a preheated 350° oven for 30 minutes, until bubbling hot.

VARIATIONS

• Instead of leftover meat, you could use some spicy Italian sausage meat, and stuff the shells with it. The sausage should be seasoned well enough so that it won't require any other seasoning. Cover it with the cheese and tomato sauce as suggested, although you may prefer to use an Italian cheese.

• Cold, previously cooked shells lend themselves to several combinations. Drain and dry on a rack after cooking. Stuff and arrange on a bed of greens. Spread a pungent vinaigrette over the stuffed shells and garnish with chopped chives and parsley.

• Suggested Stuffings for Shells

  1. Well-seasoned Shrimp Salad

  2. Crab or Lobster Salad

  3. A brightly flavored Chicken Salad

• Your salad plate may be garnished with onion rings and Niçoise olives, cherry tomatoes, and hard-boiled eggs.

Spinach Ravioli

Making ravioli is one of those skills that is perfectly simple—once you know how. Don't be put off if your first tries are messy. You might want to practice on this spinach-and-ricotta-stuffed ravioli and then, once you've got the knack, go on to a more expensive filling.

[4 to 6 servings]

1 recipe French Noodles (p. 46)

STUFFING:
2½ pounds fresh spinach, or two 10-ounce
    packages frozen spinach
1 large clove garlic
½ teaspoon nutmeg
½ cup ricotta cheese
½ teaspoon Tabasco
1 teaspoon salt

SAUCE:
½ cup butter, melted
¼ pound Gruyère cheese, grated
½ cup chopped parsley

◄ɕPrepare the pasta dough and let it rest.

Plunge the spinach into boiling water, let wilt for 1 minute, and drain. Place it in a hand towel and squeeze out all the liquid. If you use frozen spinach, defrost it and squeeze it dry in the same manner. Combine the spinach with the garlic, nutmeg, ricotta, Tabasco, and salt in the beaker of a food processor, and process until you have a smooth paste.

Roll out the pasta dough into 2 rectangular sheets. Drop tiny bits of filling, about ½ teaspoon each, at regular intervals across one sheet of pasta. Lay the second sheet over it and, using your fingertip, press down between the mounds of filling, forming squares. Cut along the edges of the squares with a pastry cutter, and seal the edges closed with the tines of a fork.

(Another method is to use a ravioli tray. Lay a sheet of dough on the tray. Then spoon bits of filling into the shallow hollows on the tray. Lay a second sheet of dough over the first, and roll over the tray with an ordinary rolling pin, forming the ravioli.

A third method is to use one of the rolling pins that is specially marked for ravioli. Roll out a large sheet of dough. Then roll over it with the marked pin. Place dabs of stuffing inside the squares on half the dough, and fold the second half of the sheet over it. Cut along the markings.

And, if you want to, there is nothing to prevent you from simply taking two sheets of pasta, cutting free-form squares with a knife, putting on the filling, and then using the fork around the edge. They'll probably look like loving-hands-at-home, but they'll taste just the same.)

To cook the ravioli: Bring a big pot of water to the boil. Drop in the ravioli, a few at a time, and cook for about 3 minutes after they float to the surface. Remove with a slotted spoon and place on a warm platter. Spoon the melted butter over the ravioli and sprinkle with cheese and parsley.

Ravioli with Sweetbread Stuffing

I wanted to do things with ravioli that weren't traditionally Italian, to use surprising seasonings and stuffings, and I think that they worked out very well. These tiny packages would make an excellent beginning to any dinner, no matter how formal.

[4 to 6 servings]

1 recipe French Noodles (p. 46)

STUFFING:
1 sweetbread
1 brain
1 chicken breast, boned
1/2 teaspoon Tabasco
2 teaspoons salt
2 egg whites
1 tablespoon fresh tarragon, or 1/2 teaspoon
  dried tarragon
3 shallots
Pinch of nutmeg

SAUCE:
1/2 cup butter
6 minced shallots
3 large sprigs tarragon, or 2 teaspoons dried
  tarragon
1/2 cup chopped parsley

Prepare the pasta dough and let it rest.

For the stuffing: Put all the ingredients into the bowl of the food processor and process well. Set the puréed mixture in a steamer and steam over boiling water for 10 to 15 minutes, stirring it now and then with a wooden spoon. Don't let it cook too long, or it will become hard. If you make the stuffing ahead of time, refrigerate it until you are ready to use it, and then put it back in the processor and blend for a few minutes to lighten it and smooth it out.

Make and cook the ravioli by one of the methods described in the preceding recipe.

To make the sauce: Melt the butter with shallots and herbs in the microwave or in a saucepan over gentle heat. Spoon over the cooked ravioli.

Crabmeat Ravioli

I have a passion for crabmeat in all its forms, and I think that this crabmeat ravioli is something quite special, very delicate and unlike any ravioli you've ever had. I used half a can of chilled, cleaned crabmeat in the stuffing, but if you have trouble finding that, canned or frozen crabmeat will do.

[4 to 6 servings]

1 recipe Basic Egg Pasta (p. 33), or ½ recipe
    French Noodles (p. 46)
½ pound jumbo lump crabmeat, or canned
    or frozen crabmeat
3 shallots
½ cup ricotta cheese
2 teaspoons dried tarragon
½ teaspoon salt
1 to 2 tablespoons yogurt, cream,
    or sour cream
¼ pound butter, melted

∾ Prepare the pasta and let it rest.

Place the crabmeat, shallots, ricotta, tarragon, and salt in the bowl of the food processor, and process until they are well blended. Add enough

yogurt or cream to make the mixture malleable.

Make and cook the ravioli by one of the methods described in the recipe for Spinach Ravioli. Place the cooked ravioli in a shallow gratin pan in an oven set at 225°. When all the ravioli are done, pour the melted butter over them, and sprinkle with grated cheese, or serve with a delicate sauce, such as the Herbed Butter Sauce on page 77.

VARIATIONS

• In place of the crabmeat, use one 7-ounce can tuna, or ½ pound shelled shrimp, or ½ pound scallops.

• For a superb celebration of spring, use ¾ pound peeled shad roe in place of the crabmeat.

Stuffed Ziti

Another wonderful way to use up leftover meat. This filling and the one for stuffed shells can be used interchangeably, but this one is a little simpler and less subtle. It's very good, too, made with ground beef and pork, just browned in a skillet before it is mixed with the seasonings.

[4 servings]

2 cups leftover meat, or 1½ pounds
   mixed ground beef and pork, browned
1 clove garlic
1 onion
Few sprigs parsley
1 egg
2 tablespoons olive oil
¼ teaspoon thyme
½ teaspoon salt
Freshly ground black pepper
½ pound large ziti
½ pound mushrooms, sliced
1 tablespoon butter
1½ cups Light Tomato Sauce (p. 73)
Grated Parmesan cheese

◆∂ Put the meat, garlic, onion, parsley, egg, olive oil, thyme, salt, and pepper in the bowl of a food processor, and process until they are well blended. If you don't mind tasting raw egg, now is the time to taste and adjust the seasoning. A lot will depend on how the meat was seasoned when it was first cooked.

Cook and drain the ziti. Using a teaspoon, fill the cooked ziti with the chopped-meat mixture. Lay them in a single layer in a shallow baking pan.

In a skillet, sauté the mushrooms in butter until they are soft, and then spoon them over the ziti. Cover with the tomato sauce, sprinkle heavily with the grated cheese, and bake for 25 minutes in a 350° oven.

Kreplach

There are 10 dozen ways of doing kreplach, and 10 times that number of people telling you that theirs is the traditional way. This one is idiotically simple, but the sage and chives make a nice combination of flavors. Use plenty of chives. I grow them in my backyard, and they're usually the first thing up in the garden, so to me they taste like springtime.

[6 servings]

1 recipe Basic Egg Pasta (p. 33)
1/2 pound ground chuck
1 tablespoon chopped fresh sage, or
   1/2 teaspoon dried sage
1 small bunch chives, minced
3 tablespoons chopped parsley
1/2 teaspoon salt
1/4 teaspoon Tabasco

Make the noodle dough, and while it rests mix the meat with the sage, chives, parsley, salt, and Tabasco. Roll out the dough in the pasta machine. Then, using a pastry wheel, cut it into 2-inch squares. Place a scant teaspoonful of filling toward one corner of each square. Moisten the edges of the square, fold one corner over another to make a triangle, and seal tightly.

Let the kreplach sit at room temperature for 30 minutes before you cook them. Drop them into salted boiling water, about 8 at a time. Cover the pot and cook each batch for about 15 minutes. Remove with a slotted spoon and add more kreplach to the pot.

Add the cooked kreplach to chicken soup, or sauté them in butter or chicken fat until they are lightly browned, and serve with pot roast or roast chicken.

Wontons

Wontons can be ill-treated or well treated, and somehow they are always delicious. In San Francisco, they fry these little dumplings in hot oil for a few minutes after they are boiled. They call them "pot stickers" because they tend to stick to the wok. If you fry them, put together a dipping sauce with soy sauce, rice vinegar, a few drops of sesame oil, and minced ginger, with some chopped cilantro floating on the top.

[6 servings]

DOUGH:
1 cup flour
1/2 teaspoon salt
1/4 teaspoon baking powder
1/2 cup ice water

1/2 pound ground pork
1 teaspoon minced ginger
4 teaspoons soy sauce
1 tablespoon chopped chives
1/2 teaspoon hot sesame oil

◄ Put the flour, salt, baking powder, and most of the water in a bowl. Mix with a fork. Use only as much water as you need to make a mixture that is soft but not wet. Form into a ball and knead on a floured surface for 5 minutes. Cover with a damp cloth and let rest for 30 minutes before rolling.

To make the stuffing: Put the pork, ginger, soy sauce, chives, and hot sesame oil in the bowl of a food processor, and let it run until everything is well mixed.

Divide the dough in half and roll one half into a thin sheet by hand or in the machine. Dust the sheet generously with cornstarch. Cut it into 3-inch squares. If you are making the squares ahead of time, you can now stack them, wrapped in aluminum foil, in the refrigerator.

To make the wontons: Place a square in front of you with a point toward you. Put a heaping ¼ teaspoon filling in the center of the square. Moisten the edges of the square and fold the point near you up to meet the point away from you, making a triangle. Press the edges together and pull the corners toward you. Press one on top of the other. The point of the wonton that is away from you should stick up, forming a kind of bonnet for the filling.

The Chinese have an interesting method for cooking wontons. They bring a great quantity of water to a boil. Then they drop in all the dumplings, turning the heat to medium. When it boils again, they add 1½ cups cold water. When it comes to a boil for the third time, they add another 1½ cups cold water. When it comes to a boil for the fourth time, they let the wontons cook for 2 minutes, then skim them out of the cooking liquid.

Tortellini

Some things are so good when you buy them that they really don't repay the effort of making them. Unless you're just bound to make everything by hand and you're awfully good with pasta, tortellini may require too much handwork, especially since they are available ready-made with such high quality. But I know that there are people who won't rest until they have mastered every skill, and it is rather fun to do these tiny dumplings, if you can get the proper twist to your fingers.

They're good served cold, in a pasta salad, but I love the classic way that Alfredo Viazzi does tortellini, with a béchamel sauce studded with prosciutto and peas. Or serve them with a good tomato sauce, or with melted butter, cheese, and lots of fresh chopped parsley. Two cups of sauce should be just right for this amount of tortellini.

[4 to 6 servings]

1 recipe Basic Egg Pasta (p. 33)
½ pound ground pork
2 tablespoons chopped fresh basil, or
    1 teaspoon dried basil
2 teaspoons fresh chives
1 large clove garlic, chopped
¼ teaspoon salt
½ teaspoon freshly ground black pepper

◄¿Make the noodle dough and, while it rests, mix the pork with the basil, chives, garlic, salt, and pepper in the food processor.

Roll out the dough by hand or machine until it is very thin. Using a round cutter 3 inches in diameter, cut the dough into as many circles as you can. Place a scant ½ teaspoon filling in the center of each circle.

Moisten the edges of the circle. Fold the dough over the filling and press the edges together to seal. Bend up a cuff along the curved edge. Then wrap the straight side of the tortellini around the tip of your forefinger, and seal the corners together.

Bring a pot of water to the boil. Drop in the tortellini, a few at a time. They will be done when they float to the top of the pot. Skim them out with a slotted spoon, and add more tortellini to the pot.

Frogs' Legs Tortelloni

These tortelloni are the creation of chef Seppi Renngli of the Four Seasons Restaurant. They have an absolutely sublime flavor, and I'm just mad about them. If you don't want to use frogs' legs, of course, you can substitute chicken, but the taste will be subtly different.

[4 to 6 servings]

1 recipe Basic Egg Pasta (p. 33)
4 slices bacon
5 shallots, chopped
1 clove garlic, finely chopped
6 fresh sage leaves, or ½ teaspoon dried sage
1 rib celery, diced
2 pounds frogs' legs
½ teaspoon salt
¼ teaspoon freshly ground black pepper
1 cup cooked spinach
3 tablespoons Parmesan cheese
2 eggs
1 quart heavy cream
5 ounces Gorgonzola cheese
1 quart chicken stock
½ pound snow peas, each cut into
   3 lengthwise strips

Prepare the pasta dough and let it rest.

Cut the bacon into 1-inch pieces and cook until they are crisp. Add the shallots, garlic, sage, and celery. Stir over the heat for a few minutes and place the frogs' legs on top. Season with salt and pepper, cover, and cook for 20 minutes on the stove top or in a 375° oven. Set aside the frogs' legs until they are cool enough to handle. When you are able to pick the meat from the bones, add it with the spinach to the frypan, and cook over high heat until all the juices have evaporated. Stir in the Parmesan cheese, taste, and correct the seasoning. Put the mixture in the bowl of the food processor, process well, and let cool.

Roll out the pasta and cut into 3-inch squares. Beat the eggs and brush the dough squares with the egg wash. Place a full teaspoonful of filling in the middle of each square. Moisten the edges, fold the dough in half, and press the edges together.

Bring the cream to a boil in a heavy saucepan and simmer until it is reduced by half. Then stir in the Gorgonzola.

In a second saucepan, bring the chicken stock to a boil. Cook the tortelloni in it for 5 minutes, adding the strips of snow peas for the last half minute of cooking. Remove the dumplings and snow peas with a slotted spoon, and add them to the cheese-cream sauce. Shake the pan until each dumpling is well coated.

Steamed Meat Packets

I like to think of this as a modern lasagne. It's so much neater than lasagne, because you don't get all the sauce running into the corners of the pan, so that someone gets cheated. Serve a platter of packets at a buffet. The meat mixture is so flavorful that you might want to pat half of it into a small loaf pan and bake it at 350° for an hour. It makes very good sandwiches.

[6 servings]

1 recipe French Noodles (p. 46)
2 pounds hamburger meat
1 pound ground pork
4 cloves garlic
2 onions
1 carrot, in chunks
1 cup soft bread crumbs
1 teaspoon dried thyme
1 tablespoon salt
1 teaspoon freshly ground black pepper
½ cup chopped Italian parsley
2 eggs
1 recipe chèvre-tomato sauce (p. 150)
1 cup grated Parmesan cheese

◀₹Prepare the pasta and let it rest.

Put the meat, vegetables, crumbs, and seasonings into the container of the food processor and process them until they are finely chopped. This may take as long as 30 seconds. Turn the mixture out into a bowl. Mix in the eggs. I like to use my hands for this process, but the squeamish can use a wooden spoon. To test the seasoning: Melt 1 tablespoon butter in a heavy skillet. Form a thin patty of the meat, and fry it in the butter for around 5 minutes, until it is crusty on the outside and brown all the way through. Adjust the seasoning.

Roll the pasta in the machine or by hand, making long strips. Using a ruler as a guide, cut the strips so that they are 5 to 5½ inches wide. There are two ways to make the packets, depending on whether they will be square or triangular. The square ones are larger, contain more filling, and make a heartier serving.

For triangular packets, roll about 1 tablespoon filling lightly into a sausage. Place it to one side, about 2 inches up from the end of the strip of dough. Lift one corner of the strip and bring it to the opposite side, forming a triangular pocket that encloses the filling. Dip your finger into a dish of water to moisten the inner edges of the triangle and press them together. Cut the triangle free with a pastry wheel and continue up the strip.

For square packets, like oversized ravioli, put 1 heaping tablespoon filling 3 inches up from the end of the strip of dough. This time, bring the whole end up to enclose the meat filling. Moisten the three open edges, press them together, and cut off the square with a pastry wheel. In both methods, seal the edges by pressing with the tines of a fork.

To cook: Put water into the bottom part of a steamer, and bring it to a boil. Oil the top of the steamer and make a single layer of packets on it. (This is one time when it is useful to have a multilayered Chinese steamer.) Cook the packets over boiling water for around 15 minutes. Take them out carefully and lay them in a buttered gratin dish. Coat with the sauce, sprinkle with Parmesan cheese, and bake for another 15 minutes in a 350° oven. They make an excellent luncheon dish with a serving of cold beans or asparagus vinaigrette.

Noodle-Eggplant Dumplings

Don't let the length of this recipe put you off. Although there are several steps involved, they can all be done well in advance of serving. Even the final assemblage can be done in the morning of the day you're going to serve the dumplings. If you find that you have leftover stuffing, by all means save it. It will be very good the next day, lightly sautéed in a little butter and served with a salad and some crisp bread.

[8 servings]

1 recipe French Noodles (p. 46)
2 pounds plum tomatoes
1/4 pound butter
1 medium onion, sliced
Salt and freshly ground black pepper
Pinch dried red-pepper flakes
1 medium-sized eggplant
1 1/2 tablespoons olive oil
1/2 cup grated Parmesan cheese
Melted butter

Mix the pasta dough and set it aside to rest. Make a tomato sauce by cooking the tomatoes with the butter and onion for 2 1/2 hours. Put them through the food processor, return to the pan, and continue to cook for another half hour, until the sauce is quite thick. Season with salt, pepper, and dried red pepper.

While the sauce cooks, cut the eggplant into cubes. Put them in a bowl and cover with salted water. After 30 minutes, pour the eggplant into a colander. Cover it with a plate on which you have put a weight: a can of soup will do. Let it sit for a while so that the excess moisture drains out of the vegetable. Pat dry with paper towels, and sauté the eggplant cubes in olive oil. Add to the tomato sauce, along with 1/4 cup of the cheese. The filling is now all ready.

Take a little more than half the ball of dough and roll it into a very thin sheet. Cut the sheet into eight 7- or 8-inch circles. (The size of these circles will depend on the size of the ramekins in which you make the dumplings. They should be large enough to cover the bottom of the ramekin and then be gathered together over the stuffing.) Put the second half of the dough through the pasta machine and cut it into fettuccine.

Bring a pot of water to the boil and drop in the pasta circles, 2 at a time. Cook them for less than a minute after the water returns to the boil. Take them out with a slotted spoon, dip them into a bowl of cold water to stop the cooking, and lay them flat on a dish towel. Cook all the circles this way. Then drop the fettuccine into the boiling water. When the water returns to the boil, drain and rinse the fettuccine and stir it into the tomato-eggplant mixture.

Butter 8 ramekins and set a single pasta circle into each one. Spoon in some of the filling and sprinkle with Parmesan cheese. Gather the dough around the filling, pleating it neatly as you do so. Secure it at the top with a toothpick. Brush melted butter over the top of the dough.

Bake in the upper third of a 425° oven for 8 minutes, until the dough is lightly browned. If you assemble the dumplings early in the day, cover them with a damp dish towel to keep them from drying out. When you are ready to bake them, bring them to room temperature, preheat the oven, and increase the baking time to 12 to 15 minutes.

COLD PASTA

Cellophane-Noodle Salad
Italian Sausage Salad
Herbed Noodle Salad
Salmon-Dill Salad with Pasta Shells
Orzo Salad
Leftover-Noodle Salad
Salade Niçoise with Pasta Shells
Macaroni Salad I
Macaroni Salad II
Piquant Salad
Codfish and Buckwheat-Noodle Salad
(with shrimp · crabmeat · scallops
or lobster)
Composed Salad

Cellophane-Noodle Salad

Cellophane noodles are bouncy and fun. They are made from powdered mung beans instead of wheat flour, and the Chinese consider them a vegetable instead of a starch. They're thin and white and transparent, and you don't cook them at all. You just soak them in hot water for about 1 hour, and they're ready to use.

[4 servings]

4 ounces cellophane noodles
2½ cups diced poached chicken
½ cup finely chopped onion or scallions
¾ cup finely chopped celery
½ cup mayonnaise
½ cup yogurt
1 tablespoon soy sauce
½ teaspoon Tabasco
Chopped parsley

Cover the cellophane noodles with hot water and soak for 1 hour. Drain.

Combine all the ingredients in a bowl. Toss well, and serve on a bed of watercress, garnished with chopped parsley.

Italian Sausage Salad

I adore all kinds of sausages; I've often said I could be happy eating nothing else. One of the simplest and best varieties is the coarsely ground Italian link sausage seasoned with garlic, basil, and anise. It's available now in most supermarkets, but if you want a real treat, make your own Italian sausage. You'll find a reliable recipe in *The New James Beard*. This salad is not a delicate nibble; it would make a wonderful picnic dish, with just a loaf of coarse bread and a really assertive red wine.

[6 servings]

6 Italian-style link sausages, sweet or hot
1/2 pound elbow macaroni or twists
4 green peppers, peeled and cut into strips
2 red onions, thinly sliced
2 cups canned kidney beans, drained
3 hard-boiled eggs, quartered
3 tablespoons chopped Italian parsley
2/3 cup olive oil
3 tablespoons wine vinegar
1 clove garlic, chopped
1/2 teaspoon salt
Freshly ground black pepper
Pinch of oregano

To cook the sausages: Prick the skins with a fork, put them in a skillet with water to cover, bring to a boil, reduce the heat, and poach for 1 minute. Drain off the water, slice the sausages into 1/2-inch lengths, and fry over medium heat in a dry skillet until browned through.

Cook and drain the pasta.

Combine the sausage, peppers, onions, macaroni, kidney beans, eggs, and parsley in a bowl. In a second bowl combine the olive oil, vinegar, garlic, salt, pepper, and oregano. Beat vigorously with a fork and pour the dressing over the salad, tossing it gently as you do so. Let everything mature in the refrigerator for a few hours.

Herbed Noodle Salad

When I made this salad on a Saturday afternoon, it tasted sharp and oily. It went into the refrigerator until the next day, when I served it at lunch. By then, the noodles had soaked up every bit of oil and vinegar, and the taste was wonderfully improved. Be sure to allow at least 12 hours to let this happen. You'll find that this is an unusually light and pleasant salad to serve as a first course, one that doesn't ruin the appetite.

[4 to 6 servings]

8 ounces Japanese buckwheat noodles
4 tablespoons olive oil
3 tablespoons sesame oil
2 tablespoons sesame-chili oil
3 tablespoons rice vinegar
2/3 cup finely chopped chives
1/2 cup chopped parsley

Cook and drain the pasta. Put the freshly drained noodles into a bowl with the olive oil, so that they won't stick together as they cool. When they are cool, add the sesame oil, sesame-chili oil, and rice vinegar. Toss well with the chives and parsley, and let stand for at least 12 hours.

Salmon-Dill Salad with Pasta Shells

Years ago, I used to make a smoked-salmon cocktail spread very much like this using lots of shallots and cream. I think that this version, with yogurt, is even better. The pasta soaks up and holds some of the wonderful shallot and salmon flavor.

[6 servings]

½ pound tiny shells or twists
¼ pound smoked salmon
¼ cup mayonnaise
¼ cup yogurt
3 tablespoons chopped shallots
Lots of finely chopped fresh dill

◀ Cook and drain the pasta.

Cut the salmon into slivers. Then toss into a dressing made of mayonnaise, yogurt, shallots, and dill. Mix with the pasta, and refrigerate the salad for several hours to let it mellow. Taste for seasoning: you may need to add pepper, but you probably won't need any salt because of the salty taste of the salmon.

Orzo Salad

I think orzo is just wonderful in place of rice in salads. It looks remarkably similar, but it doesn't seem to dissolve if you overcook it, as rice does. Instead of tongue, you might use an equal amount of diced chicken, turkey, or ham, two 7-ounce cans tuna fish, or a pound of cooked crabmeat or shrimp.

[6 servings]

1½ cups orzo
2 cups diced cooked veal or beef tongue
1 cup finely chopped scallions
1 cup thinly sliced fennel or celery
¼ cup finely chopped parsley
¾ cup mayonnaise
¼ cup yogurt
¼ teaspoon Tabasco
1 teaspoon freshly ground black pepper

◄⅝Cook and drain the orzo.

Combine it with the remaining ingredients, and toss them well, using a wooden spoon or your hands. Let the salad mellow for at least 2 hours before you use it, so that the flavors have a chance to develop.

VARIATION

• Cook and cool the orzo. While it is still warm stir in, with a fork, 3 tablespoons olive oil and 2 ounces wine vinegar. Toss well together. Combine cold orzo with 1 cup sliced radishes, 1 cup shredded cabbage, 1 cup finely chopped stuffed olives, and 8–10 finely cut anchovy filets. Add ⅔ cup olive oil, 3 tablespoons wine vinegar, and 1 or 2 crushed cloves garlic. Toss well. Serve with cold meats or fish.

Leftover-Noodle Salad

The only essentials in this recipe are the noodles and the dressing. Think of it as a pattern, one to follow when you have leftover pasta and want to do something light and bright with it. It's very good as it is, but you could empty out the refrigerator, add a little of this and that, and wind up with something even better.

[4 servings]

3 cups leftover cooked pasta of any sort,
   except one with a soupy sauce
3½-ounce can tuna, drained
1 cup chopped onion
1 cup chopped celery
½ cup yogurt
½ cup mayonnaise
1 tablespoon Dijon mustard
1 tablespoon chopped fresh dill

If there is sauce clinging to the pasta, rinse it in a colander under lots of cold water. Shake it dry, and put it in a bowl with the tuna, onion, and celery.

In a small bowl beat together the yogurt, mayonnaise, mustard, and dill. Then toss the dressing with the pasta, and let the mixture rest for at least 30 minutes at room temperature before you serve it.

VARIATION

• If you have cold boiled beef or veal or chicken add 2 cups diced (cooked boiled beef is especially good), plus 1 cup finely chopped celery, 1 cup chopped scallions, and 1 cup coarsely shredded carrots. Add garlic-scented vinaigrette to taste. Toss the salad and arrange in a bowl. Garnish with freshly sliced dill pickle and quartered hard-boiled eggs.

Salade Niçoise with Pasta Shells

Salade Niçoise must have tuna, tomato, olives, onions, and potatoes—but how they are put together is nobody's business but your own. This time, we used pasta shells instead of the usual potatoes, which seems a very pleasant way to change the formula.

[2 servings]

4 ounces small shells or other pasta
¼ cup olive oil
3 tablespoons tarragon vinegar
1 large clove garlic, chopped
4 heads Belgian endive, quartered
1 can anchovies
4 medium tomatoes, peeled and cut in wedges
3½-ounce can tuna
½ cup Greek olives
3 hard-boiled eggs, quartered
1 red onion, cut in rings
1 tablespoon capers

VINAIGRETTE:
¾ cup olive oil
3 tablespoons white-wine vinegar
½ cup coarsely cut basil leaves
2 teaspoons Worcestershire sauce
1 teaspoon freshly ground black pepper

Cook and drain the pasta. Combine the pasta shells with the olive oil, tarragon vinegar, and garlic. Cover, and marinate for 2 to 3 hours.

Place the marinated pasta in the center of an oval platter, with the endive at either end. Put the anchovies alongside the endive, and arrange the tomatoes, tuna, olives, eggs, and onion rings attractively around the pasta. Sprinkle capers over everything.

Blend the ingredients for the vinaigrette and pour over the salad just before you serve it, or pass the sauce separately in a bowl.

Macaroni Salad I

Macaroni salad is standard picnic fare in much of this country. You can do it with endless variations, adding mustard, peppers, onions, or chives. But for the greatest improvement, try making it with a homemade mayonnaise. Then you get a fresh taste, and avoid that awful three-days-old taste that you sometimes get from delicatessen macaroni salad.

[6 servings]

1 egg
2 egg yolks
1 tablespoon lemon juice or vinegar
1 teaspoon salt
¼ teaspoon freshly ground black pepper
1½ cups olive oil, or half olive
*   and half peanut oil*
6 ounces macaroni
2 teaspoons Dijon mustard
2 cloves garlic, chopped
2 medium onions, chopped
2 cups chopped celery
3 bell peppers, roasted, peeled, and sliced
3 hard-boiled eggs, sliced
¼ cup chopped parsley

⋖ Make the mayonnaise in the food processor. (To make it by hand or in the blender, you will have to adjust the proportions.) With the metal blade in place, add the egg and egg yolks, lemon juice, salt, and pepper. Process until they are blended, about 3 seconds. Continue processing as you slowly pour the oil through the feeding tube. Taste to see if it needs more vinegar, salt, or pepper. This recipe makes nearly 2 cups mayonnaise. Measure out 1 cup for the salad, and put the rest in a container, cover, and store in the refrigerator. It will be good for a week to 10 days.

Cook and drain the pasta.

Mix the mayonnaise and mustard in a large bowl. Toss in the other ingredients, blend with the dressing, and refrigerate until ready to serve.

Macaroni Salad II

A very different macaroni salad, and a recipe large enough to take with you to a picnic or a covered-dish supper. It's astonishing how the flavors dull out when the dish is chilled. The vinaigrette will seem quite tangy when it is first mixed, but when it is given a few hours to mellow, it will become blunted.

[8 servings]

1 pound elbow macaroni
4 or 5 ribs celery, thinly sliced
16 scallions, thinly sliced
2 medium carrots, shredded
2 long, preserved green chilies,
   peeled and chopped
1 cup chopped parsley
1/2 cup olive oil, or more if needed
3 tablespoons vinegar
1 tablespoon Dijon mustard
1 teaspoon salt
1/2 teaspoon freshly ground black pepper

◄ε Cook and drain the pasta. Toss the cooked macaroni with the vegetables. Make a vinaigrette by beating together the oil, vinegar, mustard, salt, and pepper, and mix into the salad. Chill before serving.

Piquant Salad

This is a substantial salad to serve at a summer luncheon with slices of cold ham or roast pork.

[4 to 6 servings]

1/2 pound pasta elbows, shells, or twists
2 tablespoons finely chopped onion
8 strips bacon, cooked, drained, and crumbled
1/2 cup mayonnaise
1/2 cup olive oil
2 tablespoons wine vinegar
2 tablespoons ketchup
1 teaspoon capers
1/2 teaspoon salt
Freshly ground black pepper
Tomatoes and hard-boiled eggs, for garnish

Cook and drain the pasta.

In a salad bowl, mix the drained pasta with the onion, bacon, and mayonnaise. In a screw-top jar, combine the olive oil, vinegar, ketchup, capers, salt, and pepper, and shake it vigorously. Pour this over the pasta mixture and mix it well: hands do a very good job here. Surround it with a border of alternating tomato wedges and hard-boiled egg quarters.

Codfish and Buckwheat-Noodle Salad

I must have Portuguese blood in me, because I love codfish so. But then, dried cod dishes are found all over the world. This salad is a steal from one that is made in central Europe, where they include lots of potatoes. I've just substituted chewy buckwheat noodles for the potatoes. I first had codfish salad on the old *Independence*. The barman in the observation bar was a Yugoslav and, if he liked you, he'd cook lunch for you every day with 8 or 10 of his favorite clients. He made the most marvelous codfish salad, and we'd eat it by the hour, along with a very brisk white wine or beer.

> 2 pounds dried salted codfish
> 1 pound Japanese buckwheat noodles
> 3/4 cup peanut oil
> 3 tablespoons vinegar
> 1 tablespoon Dijon mustard
> 3 tablespoons soy sauce
> 2 large cloves garlic, finely chopped
> 12 shallots, chopped, or enough
>   chopped onion to make 1 cup
> 1/2 cup chopped parsley

The night before you plan to cook the fish, put it to soak in cold water. Change the water several times to soften the fillets and remove the salt. When you are ready to cook the fish, drain it, put it in a saucepan, and cover it with fresh water. Bring to a boil and simmer 15 minutes, or until tender. Drain, and set aside.

Cook and drain the noodles.

Make a dressing of the oil, vinegar, mustard, soy sauce, garlic, and shallots. Break the fish apart with a fork or your fingers. Mix it with the noodles, the vinaigrette, and the chopped parsley. Serve on a bed of salad greens, garnished with lemon wedges and sprigs of parsley.

VARIATION

• Instead of the codfish, use 1 pound shrimp, crabmeat, or scallops, or the equivalent amount of lobster meat. If you use fresh fish, you will not, of course, soak it before you cook it, and will probably cut down the cooking time, depending on the thickness of the fish.

Composed Salad

Composed salads are so much fun. You do a still life, a great picture on a platter, and then everyone eats what he wants. This, by the way, is the answer to people who say that noodles are fattening. The only calories worth counting in this composed salad are in the olive oil and the duck skin. I used Chinese cellophane or transparent noodles, made of mung-bean flour.

[8 servings]

3 ounces cellophane noodles
4 pounds mushrooms
3 shallots, finely chopped
1/2 cup olive oil
1/4 cup wine vinegar
1 tablespoon Dijon mustard
1 teaspoon salt
1 teaspoon freshly ground black pepper
1 duck breast, cooked and skinned
2 to 3 heads Boston lettuce
2 heads Bibb lettuce
2 bunches scallions, shredded
4 to 6 beets, cooked, peeled, and sliced
1/4 pound sugar snap peas

VINAIGRETTE:
1 teaspoon coarse salt
1/2 teaspoon freshly ground black pepper
1 teaspoon Dijon mustard
2 tablespoons wine vinegar
1/2 cup fruity olive oil
Chopped parsley

◄୬ Begin by preparing the transparent noodles. These must be soaked before they are cooked. Because they overcook in no time at all, we've had to work out a way to keep them from melting into jelly. Cover the noodles with cold water and let them soak for an hour. Drain them, return them to the bowl, cover with boiling water, and let them cool in the water for 30 minutes. Drain and set aside.

Wipe the mushrooms with damp paper towels. Remove the stems, and put them aside to use in a soup or stew. Put the caps in a bowl with the shallots, olive oil, vinegar, mustard, salt, and pepper. Mix well, cover, and marinate for at least 1 hour.

Remove the duck skin from the meat, and slice both skin and meat into thin strips. Put the meat aside and fry the strips of skin in very hot oil in a skillet until they are crisp. Set the pieces aside to drain on a paper towel.

Now arrange the lettuce leaves on a large platter. On them, arrange the drained marinated mushrooms, the noodles, scallions, beets, duck breast, and peas. The whole point of a composed salad is its composition, so use all your skill in the arrangement.

You can prepare the salad ahead to this point. Just before you serve it, mix a vinaigrette of salt, pepper, Dijon mustard, vinegar, and oil. Spoon it over the salad, and garnish with strips of crisp duck skin and with chopped parsley.

Lemon Juice and Pepper
Garlic and Oil
Parsley and Cheese
Pasta and Peppers

SMALL
SAUCINGS

Yogurt Sauce
Cottage Cheese
Cucumber Salad
Duxelles
Quick Cream and Tomato Sauce
Ham and Peas
Anchovy Sauce
Mushroom Sauce
Raisin and Pignoli Sauce
Quick Tuna Sauce
Smoked Salmon and Scotch
Olives
Oysters
Canned Tomato Sauce

When I was testing the pasta recipes for this book I very often found myself with an embarrassment of riches at lunchtime. The simplest solution was to put the hot cooked noodles in a bowl, drop in a nugget of unsalted butter, and toss it with whatever cheese I had in the refrigerator.

But there were other solutions that were nearly as simple, and were often more delicious than prepared, long-cooked sauces. For example, I might melt the butter into the pasta and then simply grind a good deal of coarsely cracked peppercorns over it. Almost any fresh herb melted in butter was good. Chopped parsley, butter, and minced garlic made a sublime sauce. And another lunch of pasta, herbs, and butter became the inspiration for the tarragon-shallot-butter sauce on page 77.

The point is that you need never be at a loss for something good to eat if you have some pasta and the resources of an ordinary kitchen. I remember one memorable meal that Marion Cunningham and I put together at La Costa, where we were giving a series of cooking demonstrations. We didn't want to eat at the spa, and we were too tired to go out to dinner. We hung around until it got late, and then we tore down to the little local grocery shop and found, to our dismay, that it was closed. Back to our demonstration kitchen we went and surveyed what we had on hand. We found a package of imported spaghettini and a couple of cans of *salsa*, the spicy onion, pepper, and green tomato sauce that is used in Mexican cooking. We cooked the pasta, dumped the *salsa*, cold, on the steaming hot spaghettini, tossed it all together, and to this day Marion claims that it's the best noodle dish she's ever had.

I've never been the sort who knew on Monday what he wanted to eat on Tuesday. Or, for that matter, who knew at three what he wanted for supper at eight. That's why I've found pasta such a resource for spontaneous, last-minute meals.

It's endless, for example, what you can do with pasta and fresh vegetables. (Even potatoes, as on page 86; even beans, as on page 90.) I might sauté broccoli florets in olive oil with garlic and pour it over shells. Stir-fry broccoli stems in peanut oil, season them with ginger and soy sauce, and serve them on a bed of cellophane noodles. Or steam the broccoli, add it to canned tomato sauce with a little cream and a good dash of Tabasco, and serve it over penne.

Here, then, is a collection of ideas that I hardly think of as recipes, but rather as last-minute inspirations for using pasta. Each one began with a quick review of what I had on hand that day in the cupboard or in the refrigerator. Each one made a gratifying meal. But then, of course, I love pasta.

Lemon Juice and Pepper

I haven't eaten baked potatoes with butter or salt for years. Instead, I squeeze on some lemon juice and then add a lot of freshly ground black pepper. If you don't want to have any oil with your pasta, there's no reason you can't treat it similarly.

Garlic and Oil

Nobody ever has to dine badly if he has olive oil, garlic, and fresh pepper. Heat ½ cup oil in a saucepan with 4 cloves finely chopped garlic. When the garlic is soft, but not brown, pour the scented oil over ½ pound of freshly cooked pasta, and grind lots of fresh pepper on top.

Parsley and Cheese

Melt a stick of butter with a clove of garlic. Then put a bunch of parsley into the bowl of the processor with a big chunk of cheese, and process well. Put some freshly drained pasta into the butter and immediately stir in the parsley and cheese, which should melt beautifully into the butter.

Pasta and Peppers

One day I found myself ready for lunch with nothing promising on hand except some fresh pasta and a bowl in the refrigerator full of roasted bell peppers in a vinaigrette sauce. I put the peppers and sauce in the processor and served the purée over the hot pasta. But I could also have sliced the peppers into slivers, perhaps added some scallions, and poured that with the vinaigrette over the pasta.

Yogurt Sauce

It's not at all traditional, but I've taken a liking to yogurt served with pasta. I make a luncheon salad by mixing cooked noodles with a cup of yogurt into which I stir about ¼ cup parsley, 2 tablespoons chopped chives, and some tarragon leaves, then let it all cool to room temperature.

Cottage Cheese

A friend tells me that the happiest meals of his childhood were in his German grandmother's kitchen, where he watched her cut out wide egg noodles, and then was served a bowl of the freshly cooked noodles mixed with cold cottage cheese sprinkled with cinnamon-sugar.

Cucumber Salad

I can see an icy-cold dish of cucumbers and onion in vinegar or yogurt tossed with hot pasta.

Duxelles

This delicious mushroom paste is used in stuffings, omelets, crêpes, or simply spread on thin toast for an appetizer. I don't suggest that you make it up for a pasta sauce, but if you have some duxelles in the refrigerator, you could well use it for an instant sauce. For the recipe, see *The New James Beard*, page 535. To use it as a sauce for pasta, spoon off about ½ cup of the paste. Warm it in a heavy pan and thin it with some cream until it is the proper consistency.

Quick Cream and Tomato Sauce

I can't deny that this is best when it's made with homemade tomato sauce. But, on the other hand, if you find yourself with a can of undistinguished commercially made tomato sauce, here's a way to turn it into something special. Heat the tomato sauce with the juice of half an orange, a dash of Tabasco, and about ¼ cup heavy cream. Warm through and pour over hot noodles.

Ham and Peas

Very simple. Pour a cup of heavy cream into a saucepan. Let it cook down and thicken slightly, and add some peas and bits of ham. Pour over hot noodles and sprinkle on quite a lot of grated cheese.

Anchovy Sauce

Everyone has a can of anchovies in his cupboard. Drain the oil into a measuring cup, and add enough olive oil to make ¼ cup plus 2 tablespoons oil altogether. Pour the oil into a saucepan with 2 cloves chopped garlic and the anchovies. Heat them all with 2 tablespoons hot water. Pour over the pasta and sprinkle with lots of chopped parsley.

Mushroom Sauce

What could be better? Sauté a lot of sliced mushrooms in butter with just a hint of garlic. Toss with the pasta and add lots of chopped chives.

Raisin and Pignoli Sauce

Made in minutes, if you have pignoli on hand. If you don't, don't despair: almonds will do in a pinch. Heat ¾ cup olive oil with 4 cloves garlic, chopped fine. Add ½ cup nuts and ½ cup raisins, and heat through. Serve over pasta, sprinkled with lots of fresh pepper and chopped parsley.

Quick Tuna Sauce

Warm ½ cup olive oil with a clove of garlic. Dump in a 7-ounce can of tuna, and break it up with a fork. Then add a lot of chopped parsley, heat through, and pour over the pasta. Add a few chopped Greek olives, if you have them.

Smoked Salmon and Scotch

I used to make this years ago. Warm some heavy cream with a good lump of butter. When it has cooked down a little, pour in a splash of Scotch. Let it heat through and pour over the noodles. Then toss in as much smoked salmon, cut into shreds, as you have. If you don't have smoked salmon, do it with canned kippers or smoked sturgeon.

Olives

Take some of the lovely black Greek olives, mix them with a little garlic and olive oil and scallions, and pour them over pasta. Green olives will do, too.

Oysters

Take freshly opened oysters (or the opened oysters that you buy from a reputable fishman). Toss them briefly with hot melted butter and pour them into a bowl of pasta. The heat from the noodles will continue to cook them. Serve with lemon wedges.

Canned Tomato Sauce

In the best of all possible worlds all tomato sauce would be freshly made. But this is not the best of all possible worlds, and sometimes that extra 20 minutes is just too long to spend on preparing dinner. That's why it's wise to have some canned tomato sauce in your pantry.

These sauces are as useful as canned tomatoes. Some are abysmally bad, while others are better, frankly, than the fresh sauces that some people would make. The packing companies are often able to get better tomatoes than we do. And there are many small companies around the country that package really high-quality sauces. Here in New York, for example, Aunt Millie's puts out three or four varieties of tomato sauce that are more than acceptable, that are really damned good.

As for the bad ones, you can always dress them up. Take a canned sauce as a starting point. Then add some browned chopped meat; or leftover meat and gravy; or a can of tuna and some parsley. Put in some mushrooms sautéed in butter. Pour in some cream: that helps a lot. Add herbs. Keep on tasting. Use your imagination.

DESSERTS

Macaroni Pudding
Noodle Pudding

Macaroni Pudding

Pasta for dessert? What a wicked thought! Now that we have had our noodles in soup, as appetizers, with meat and fish and eggs and salad, let's pay a final tribute to excess and have a wonderful macaroni pudding. This is a very old English recipe that probably dates at least from the eighteenth century. And you can trust the English when it comes to sweets—it's awfully good.

[4 servings]

1 cup elbow macaroni
½ cup raisins
¼ cup rum
2 cups milk
4 egg yolks
½ cup sugar
1 teaspoon vanilla or almond extract

❧ Cook and drain the pasta.

Cover the raisins with rum and set them aside to soak.

Put the milk in a heavy saucepan over medium-high heat. When it is nearly scalded, just before tiny bubbles appear around the edge of the pan, begin to beat the egg yolks and sugar in the electric mixer. Keep the mixer going while you pour in the hot milk. Add the vanilla, and pour into a baking dish. Stir in the macaroni and the drained raisins, and bake in a 350° oven for 45 minutes. The pudding will continue to set as it cools, but it is wonderful hot, too.

Noodle Pudding

This famous Jewish specialty looks and tastes like a dessert. It is usually served in a kosher meal with the main course as a sweet starch, something on the order of candied sweet potatoes. I've saved it for the end of the book because I really enjoy it more as a dessert.

I've had two kinds of noodle pudding. One is made with cottage cheese and sour cream and goes with "dairy" meals, and the other is made with fruit and goes with meat meals. When I adapted the recipe, I used butter in place of the traditional vegetable oil or margarine, and I think it adds to the quality.

[4 to 6 servings]

1/2 pound broad noodles
4 eggs, lightly beaten
1/4 cup sugar
1/4 teaspoon ginger
1/2 cup butter, melted
1 teaspoon salt
2 cooking apples, peeled and diced
1/3 cup raisins
1/2 cup dried apricots, cut in sixths
1/2 teaspoon cinnamon mixed with
    2 teaspoons sugar

❧ Cook and drain the noodles.

Mix them with everything but the cinnamon-sugar. Pour the mixture into a buttered 2-quart baking dish, sprinkle the top with the cinnamon-sugar, dot with more butter, and bake at 350° for 40 minutes.

Food Suppliers

NEW YORK

Balducci's
424 Sixth Ave.
New York, N.Y. 10009
Tel: (212) 673–2600

Some imported pastas
Prosciutto
Sausages
Oils

Dean & Deluca
121 Prince St.
New York, N.Y. 10012
Tel: (212) 254–7774

Cheeses
Choice oils
Imported pastas
Prosciutto
Sausages
Excellent pots

Ideal Cheese Co.
1205 Second Ave.
New York, N.Y. 10021
Tel: (212) 688–7579

Domestic and imported cheeses

Manganaro's
488 Ninth Ave.
New York, N.Y. 10018
Tel: (212) 563–5331

Semolina
Pancetta
Imported pastas
Cheeses—caciocavallo
and other
Italian cheeses

H. Roth & Sons
1577 First Ave.
New York, N.Y. 10028
Tel: (212) 734–1110

Flours, seasonings, and unusual
equipment (spätzle machine)

Wing Fat & Co.
35 Mott St.
New York, N.Y. 10013
Tel: (212) 962–0423

Fresh Chinese noodles (refrigerated)
Lemon grass, fresh ginger
Skimmers

CALIFORNIA

The Chinese Grocer
209 Post St.
San Francisco, CA. 94108
Tel: (800) 227–3320

Chinese noodles, seasonings, and
equipment

Jurgensens
Chain of stores throughout Los
Angeles, Santa Barbara, and
Pasadena areas. Check local
directories for addresses.

Flours and cheeses

Mandarin Delight Market
1024 Stockton St.
San Francisco, CA. 94108
Tel: (415) 781-4650
Chinese products and seasonings

The Perfect Pan
897 1st St.
Encinatas, CA 92024
Both food and equipment

The Perfect Pan
La Jolla Village Square
8657 Villa La Jolla Dr.
La Jolla, CA 92037
Both food and equipment

The Mission Hills Perfect Pan
4040 Goldfinch
San Diego, CA 92103
Equipment

Williams-Sonoma
576 Sutter St.

San Francisco, CA. 94102
Tel: (415) 982-0295
Williams-Sonoma
Mail Order Dept.
P.O. Box 3792
San Francisco, CA. 94119
Pasta machines
Mixers of all kinds
Fine oils
Rolling pins
Herbs

Yee Sing Chong Co., Inc.
966 North Hill St.
Los Angeles, CA. 90012
Tel: (213) 626-9619
Great selection of Chinese cleavers

The Ying Co.
1120 Stockton St.
San Francisco, CA. 94133
Tel: (415) 982-2188
Chinese products

PORTLAND

Anzen Japanese Foods & Imports
736 North East Union Ave.
Portland, OR. 97232
Tel: (503) 233-5111
Japanese noodles and seasonings

CHICAGO

Oriental Food Market & Cooking School
2801 West Howard
Chicago, IL. 60645
Tel: (312) 274-2826
Both Japanese and Chinese noodles, seasonings, etc.

INDEX

A

acini di pepe
in Pasta and Cheese Roll in Tomato
Sauce, 154–5
all-purpose flour, 6
almonds
in Nutted Chicken-Rice Noodle
Casserole, 112–13
Alsatian Riesling
in Coq au Riesling over Noodles,
116–17
anchovies
in Orzo Salad, 192
in Pasta with Sardines, 102
in Salade Niçoise with Pasta Shells,
194
Anchovy-Spinach Sauce, 75
Andoh, Elizabeth, 50
angel hair
in Pasta Primavera, 78
in Savory Tongue with Fine Noodles,
139
with Spinach-Anchovy Sauce, 75
Angel Hair with Golden Caviar, 96
Angel-Hair Soufflé, 163
Appenzeller
definition of, 24
apples
in Noodle Pudding, 215
apricots
in Noodle Pudding, 215
Artichoke and Chicken-Liver Sauce,
122–3
Asiago
description of, 21
asparagus
in Pasta Primavera, 78
Asparagus with Spaghettini, 80
At Home with Japanese Cooking

(Elizabeth Andoh), 50
Aunt Millie's tomato sauces, 211
Avocado Pasta, 92–3

B

bacon
in Beach Pâté, 132–3
in Frogs' Legs Tortelloni, 180–81
in Pasta with Beans, 90–91
in Piquant Salad, 197
bamboo shoots
in Soft Noodles Sautéed, 144
Barbara Kafka's Buckwheat Noodles, 49
basil (fresh)
in Pesto Sauce, 72–3
in Potato Gnocchi, 61
Basil Lasagne, 157
Basil Pasta, 45
Bass, Striped, with Fettuccine, 99
Beach Pâté, 132
bean sprouts
in Broiled Duck with Rice Noodles,
124–5
in Soft Noodles Sautéed, 143–4
beans
dried
kidney, in Italian Sausage Salad,
189
green
in Pasta Primavera, 78
Beans with Pasta, 90–91
Béchamel Sauce, 136–7
with Lasagne, 136–7
in Macaroni and Cheese, 156
in Orzo Soufflé, 160–61
beef
chuck
ground in Beach Pâté, 132–3

beef, chuck (*cont'd*)
  ground in Kreplach, 175
  ground in Lasagne, 136–8
  flank steak
    in Soft Noodles Sautéed, 144
  hamburger meat
    in Steamed Meat Packets, 182–3
  lean
    ground in Pastitsio for a Party,
      126–7
  leftover
    boiled, cold, in Leftover Noodle
      Salad, 193
    ground in Stuffed Ziti, 174
  short ribs Chilied over Corn
    Macaroni, 134
  tongue
    with Fine Noodles, 139
    in Orzo Salad, 192
Beef and Scallops with Cellophane
  Noodles, 131
beer
  in Barbara Kafka's Buckwheat
    Noodles, 49
  what to drink with pasta, 27
Beet Pasta, 45
beets
  in Composed Salad, 200–201
Bel Paese, 151
Bialetti, 7
Bloomingdale's (New York)
  for fresh pasta, 5
Blue de Bresse
  description of, 24
blue cheese
  with spaghetti and tomatoes, 150
blue-veined cheese, 24
Bolles, de, 3
Boursin, 21
Bowknots with Chicken Stir-Fry,
  118–19
bows
  with Braised Onion Sauce, 76
brain

in Ravioli with Sweetbread
    Stuffing, 170–71
Bread Noodles, 52–3, *ill.* 52, 53
Brie (leftover), 20
broccoli
  suggested uses with pasta, 204
buckwheat flour
  in Barbara Kafka's Noodle Casserole,
    49
buckwheat noodles
  Chinese, 3
  Japanese, 3
    in Codfish Salad, 198–9
    in Herbed Noodle Salad, 190
Buckwheat Pasta, 45
Bugialli, Giuliano, xi
Bulgarian Shredded Noodles, 54–5

C

cabbage
  in Orzo Salad, 192
Cabbage with Noodles, 88
Caciocavallo
  description of, 21
  in Bulgarian Shredded Noodles,
    54–5
  in Potato Gnocchi, 60–61
  in Spaghetti Carbonara, 152–3
Caerphilly
  description of, 26
Cantal
  description of, 26
capers
  in Piquant Salad, 197
  in Salade Niçoise with Pasta Shells,
    194
  in Swordfish-Olive Pasta, 101
carrots
  in Beach Pâté, 132–3
  in Leftover Noodle Salad, 193
  in Macaroni Salad, 11, 196
  in Sautéed Vegetables with Spätzle,
    79

equipment (*cont'd.*)
rolling machine, 8
rolling pin, 7, *ill.* 7
tongs, 12, *ill.* 12
tortellini stamps, 10
wooden paddles, 12

F

farmer cheese
description of, 22
fennel
in Orzo Salad, 192
in Pasta with Sardines, 102–3
feta cheese, 129
fettuccine
in Noodle-Eggplant Dumplings, 185
Fettuccine with Pesto and Potatoes, 86
Fettuccine with Striped Bass, 99
with flounder fillets, 99
Fettuccine with Zucchini, 81
fish
anchovy(ies)
in Orzo Salad, 192
in Pasta with Sardines, 102
in Salade Niçoise with Pasta Shells,
194
Spinach Sauce, 75
Bass, Striped, with Fettuccine, 99
Codfish and Buckwheat Noodle
Salad, 198–9
flounder fillets with Fettuccine, 99
kippers (canned) and Scotch, 210
perch with Fettuccine, 99
roe
Angel Hair with Golden Caviar, 96
shad in Stuffed Ravioli, 173
Sardines with Pasta, 102–3
smelts with Pasta, 102–3
smoked sturgeon and Scotch, 210
See also seafood; shrimp; tuna fish
flank steak
in Soft Noodles Sautéed, 144

flounder
fillets with Fettuccine, 99
flour
all-purpose, 6
buckwheat
in Barbara Kafka's Buckwheat
Noodles, 49
in Buckwheat Pasta, 45
durum wheat
in commercial pasta, 2, 5
cooking time, 11–12
in French Noodles, 46
in homemade pasta, 5–6
hard wheat
in Spätzle, 56
pasta, 5
semolina, 6
in French Noodles, 46
in Spätzle, 56
strong wheat, 5
Udon
in Udon Noodles, 50–51
Fontina, 20, 151
Danish, 26
Italian, 25
Four Seasons Restaurant (New York),
56, 180
fraisage, 46–7, *ill.* 46–7
French Noodles, 46–7, *ill.* 46–7
in Eggplant Dumplings, 184–5
in Ravioli with Sweetbread Stuffing,
170–71
in Steamed Meat Packets, 182–3
Frogs' Legs Tortelloni, 180–81
funghini
in Beach Pâté, 132–3

G

game hens
with Riesling over Noodles, 117
garlic
in Gremolata, 140

garlic *(cont'd.)*
   in Pasta with Parsley Pesto, 85 ·
   in Pesto Sauce, 72–3
   in Spaghetti with Clam Sauce, 97
   in Spaghettini with Asparagus, 80
Garlic and Oil, 206
General Mills, 6
ginger (fresh)
   in Soft Noodles Sautéed, 143–4
   in Udon Noodle Soup, 67–8
Gizzards with Pasta, 121
Gloucester, Double,
   description of, 26
gluten, 6
Gnocchi à la Parisienne, 146–7
Gnocchi, Potato, 60–61
Gnocchi Verdi, 62–3
goat cheese
   in Pasta con Quatro Formaggi, 151
   See also Chèvre
Golden Pasta, 45
Gorgonzola
   description of, 24
   in Frogs' Legs Tortelloni, 180–81
   in Pasta con Quatro Formaggi, 151
Gouda, aged
   description of, 21
Green Pasta, 45
Gremolata
   on Ossi Buchi with Orzo, 140
Gruyère
   in Angel-Hair Soufflé, 163
   description of, 24
   in Lasagne, 136–8
   in Orzo Soufflé, 160–62
   in Pasta con Quatro Formaggi, 151
   in Potato Gnocchi, 61
   in Spinach-Mushroom Casserole,
     87
   in Stuffed Shells, 166–7
   in Whole-Wheat-Noodle Casserole,
     158
guinea hens
   with Riesling and Noodles, 117

H

ham
   diced in Orzo Salad, 192
   Smithfield in Spaghetti Carbonara,
     152–3
   smoked in Gnocchi à la Parisienne,
     146–7
Ham and Peas on hot noodles, 208
hamburger meat
   in Steamed Meat Packets, 182–3, *ill.*
     183
Havarti, Cream
   description of, 26
Hazan, Marcella, xi, 4, 7
Herbed Butter Sauce, 77
Herbed Noodle Salad, 190
herbs. *See individual names*

I

Ideal Cheese Shop (New York), 17
Independence (ship), 198
Italian Sausage Salad, 189

J

jack cheese
   in Verna Ross's Baked Chicken
     Goulash and Spaghetti, 107
Japanese noodles
   buckwheat, 3
     in Codfish Salad, 198–9
     in Herbed Salad, 190
   Udon, 3
     with Peking Curry-Tomato Sauce,
      130
     Soup, 67
   wheat
     with Peking Curry-Tomato Sauce,
      130
Jarlsberg
   description of, 24

Jerusalem artichoke pasta, 3
Jones, Evan, 20, 151
  World of Cheese, 151

K

Kafka, Barbara, 49, 131
  Barbara Kafka's Buckwheat Noodles,
    49
Kashkaval
  description of, 22
Kasseri
  in Leon Lianides's Leg of Lamb with
    Orzo, 128–9
ketchup
  in Piquant Salad, 197
kippers (canned) with noodles and
    Scotch, 210
Kitchen Aid, 8
kneading
  basic dough, 34
  by foot, 50, *ill.* 50
Kreplach, 175

L

lamb
  ground in Pastitsio for a Party, 126–7
  Leon Lianides's Leg with Orzo, 128–9
Lang, George, 41
Lasagne, 136–8, *ill.* 137, 138
Lasagne, Basil, 157
leeks
  in Tagliarini Verdi al Guanciale, 145
  in Udon Noodle Soup, 67–8
Leftover Noodle Salad, 193
Lemon Juice and Pepper on pasta, 206
lemon zest
  in Gremolata, 140
lettuce
  Bibb, in Composed Salad, 200–201
  Boston, in Composed Salad, 200–201

Lianides, Leon, 126, Leg of Lamb, 128–9
linguine
  in Pasta Primavera, 78
Linguine with Tomato-Shrimp Sauce,
    98
lobster
  with Buckwheat-Noodle Salad, 199
  salad as stuffing for shells, 167

M

macaroni
  with Braised Onion Sauce, 76
  elbow
    in Italian Sausage Salad, 189
    in Pasta with Beans, 90–91
    in Pasta with Sardines, 102–3
    in Pastitsio for a Party, 126–7
Macaroni and Cheese, 156
Macaroni, Corn, with Chilied Short
    Ribs, 134–5
Macaroni with Mustard Cheese, 159
Macaroni Pudding, 214
Macaroni Salad I, 195
Macaroni Salad II, 196
Madeira
  in Braised Onion Sauce, 76
  in Gnocchi à la Parisienne, 146–7
  in Spinach-Mushroom Casserole, 87
Madeleine Restaurant (Paris), 146
malfatti, 62
mayonnaise (homemade)
  in Macaroni Salad I, 195
meat
  -balls in Lasagne, 136–8
  leftover
    in Stuffed Shells, 166–7
    in Stuffed Ziti, 174
  and Tomato Sauce on Penne or Ziti,
    106
  See also beef; lamb; pork; veal
Monterey Jack
  description of, 25

U

Udon Noodles, 50–51, *ill.* 50
Udon Noodle Soup, 67–8

V

veal
    cold, in Leftover Noodle Salad, 193
    shanks, in Ossi Buchi with Orzo,
        140
    tongue
        in Orzo Salad, 192
        Savory, with Fine Noodles, 139
vegetable(s)
    dishes, 79–93
    sauces, 72–8
    See also under individual names
Vegetable-Noodle Casserole, 89
Vegetables Sautéed with Spätzle, 79
Verna Ross's Baked Chicken Goulash
        and Spaghetti, 107
Viazzi, Alfredo, 178
vinaigrette
    on Codfish and Buckwheat-Noodle
        Salad, 198–9
    on Composed Salad, 200–201
    on Pasta and Peppers, 206
    on Salade Niçoise with Pasta Shells,
        194
    on cold Stuffed Shells, 167
vodka, 27, 96

W

wagon wheels
    with Braised Onion Sauce, 76
    with Old-Fashioned Chicken Fricasse,
        108–9

walnuts
    in Pasta with Parsley Pesto, 85
    in Pesto, 73
Whole-Wheat-Noodle Casserole, 158
Whole-Wheat Pasta, 45
wine
    to drink with Pasta, 27
    white
        in Coq au Riesling, 116
        in Pork with Sauerkraut Noodles,
            142
        in Spaghetti with Clam Sauce, 97
Wontons, 176–7
    Chinese method, 177
World of Cheese (Evan Jones), 151

Y

yogurt
    in Leftover Noodle Salad, 193
    in Salmon-Dill Salad with Pasta
        Shells, 191
    in Whole-Wheat-Noodle Casserole,
        158
Yogurt Sauce, 207

Z

ziti
    in Pasta con Quatro Formaggi, 151
    in Pastitsio for a Party, 126–7
    ribbed in Swordfish-Olive Pasta, 101
    with Sausage-Tomato Sauce, 141
Ziti with Tomato-Ground Meat Sauce,
        106
Ziti, Stuffed, 174
zucchini
    in Sautéed Vegetables with Spätzle,
        79
    in Vegetable-Noodle Casserole, 89
Zucchini with Fettuccine, 81

A NOTE ABOUT THE AUTHOR

James Beard was born in Portland, Oregon, and it was there that his lifelong love affair with good food started. His first cookbook, *Hors d'Oeuvre and Canapés*, was published in 1930; since then he wrote nineteen books on food, including *The James Beard Cookbook*, for years a best-selling paperback; the much-honored *James Beard's American Cookery*; the companion volumes, *Theory & Practice of Good Cooking*, which explores all the whys and wherefores of cooking as he has taught his students, and *The New James Beard*, which puts into practice what he preached. His highly popular *Beard on Bread* covers the world of bread in much the same way that this book treats pasta. Some twenty-five years ago Mr. Beard started giving cooking lessons in what later became the kitchen of the restaurant Lutèce, which was the beginning of his famous cooking school later located in his own brownstone in New York's Greenwich Village. Well-known throughout this country as a cooking authority, Mr. Beard traveled widely and taught and demonstrated cooking in many parts of the country.